# THE ACTOR'S ART

## A PRACTICAL TREATISE

ON

## STAGE DECLAMATION, PUBLIC SPEAKING, AND DEPORTMENT,

FOR THE USE OF

### Artists, Students, and Amateurs,

INCLUDING

*A Sketch on the History of the Theatre, from the Greeks to the Present Time,*

BY

## GUSTAVE GARCIA,

PROFESSOR OF SINGING AND DECLAMATION AT THE ROYAL ACADEMY OF MUSIC,
AND THE LONDON ACADEMY OF MUSIC;
PROFESSOR OF SINGING AT THE ROYAL COLLEGE OF MUSIC, AND THE
GUILDHALL SCHOOL OF MUSIC, ETC., ETC.

ILLUSTRATED BY A. FORESTIER.

SECOND EDITION.

'Action, *and* utterance, *and* the power of speech."—SHAKESPEARE'S *Julius Cæsar*

*All Rights Reserved.*

LONDON:
MESSRS SIMPKIN, MARSHALL, & CO.,
4 STATIONERS' HALL COURT.
1888.

TO

# HENRY IRVING,

THIS SHORT EXPOSITION OF

## THE ACTOR'S ART

IS DEDICATED.

# PREFACE.

———✳———

A N experience of many years in teaching singing and acting, has convinced me, that the latter as well as the former art can be reduced, like grammar, to a series of rules; and in the present work will be found, briefly, but plainly and practically recorded, the result of my experience. Every person who comes before the public, either in the capacity of a singer, an actor, a preacher, or a barrister, must study, under particularly different aspects, the management of the voice, with the rules of elocution and action. Each of these branches forms a special study. The observations here offered in the first instance to singers and actors, may also have some interest for preachers and barristers, inasmuch as they treat of the voice and elocution.

It would manifestly be impossible to handle the subject exhaustively within the limits I have been obliged to prescribe to myself, in a treatise of this kind; but it has been my endeavour to give the results of my observations and experience in a plain practical manner, that will not, I trust, be without its use to the student.

# SUMMARY OF CONTENTS.

# INTRODUCTORY.

" Action, *and* utterance, *and* the power of speech, to stir men's blood."

CICERO said that memory was the treasure of the fool. In this he was right; for the intelligent man does not consider it enough to commit a few sentences to memory; every word that he learns must be thoroughly understood, every sentiment must become part of his own consciousness ;—for the effect of spoken words depends in a great measure on the mode of delivery.

To declaim with effect, every sentence must be uttered as if from a mind fully permeated with the subject and confident of its own power, so that no hesitation or appearance of uncertainty may weaken the force of delivery or impede the flow of words.

The voice must be thoroughly kept under control and pitched in a medium tone, so that its power may be increased when necessary without straining, and subdued without becoming weak or inaudible. All the different shades of sentiment must remain musical—that is, sonorous and vibrating in quality. Speakers or actors who lose control over their voice, or indulge in exuberant gesticulation, fail to be impressive. A gradation must be strictly observed towards an increase or decrease of emotion. So soon as the climax point of the passage has been reached, by gradually increasing the pitch of the voice, the speaker must contrast his effect by immediately lowering the pitch either gradually or suddenly. Pathetic passages will be all the more impressive if the voice sinks low.

A speaker who delivers his words flowingly and with a musical voice adds a great charm to the work of which he is the interpreter, and enchants the listener. On the contrary, a lachrymose, gloomy or spasmodic tone—a monotonous rhythm, such as is caused by putting a jerky accent, on every alternate word or syllable—or dropping the voice at the end of the words or lines ; or a mechanical elocution—all defects caused by an insensibility to rhythmical modulation—produce in the hearer a sense of extreme fatigue and annoyance.

Cardinal Maury said—" Orators should vary the inflection of their voices with each rhetorical figure, and their intonation with every paragraph. Let them imitate the simple and impressive accents of nature in delivery as well as in composition. In the flowing stream of utterance blend pauses, which are always striking, when cautiously used and timed." Thus a striking effect is produced by the pauses in the lines from Gray's " Bard," in which the lament of the minstrel is interrupted by his astonishment, on seeing the spectral forms of his " lost companions " on the opposite rocks :—

> " No more I weep. They do not sleep.
>   On yonder cliff—a grisly band—
> I see them sit—they linger yet—
>   avengers of their native land."

" Such," continues the Cardinal, " are the innocent artifices by which a Christian Orator may insure the success of his mission. Roundness and music in the voice, expression in the face, graceful and energetic actions of the body, are the natural gifts which harmonise with the power of the intellect." Cicero declared that with the features of the face, the actions of the body, and the voice, all the sentiments of the soul could be expressed. No one could be an Orator who was deficient in these faculties. Buffon speaks of "Un ton véhément et pathétique, des gestes expressifs, des paroles rapides et sonnantes."

Tragedians, comedians, singers and public speakers must bear in mind that fulness of sound, modulation of the voice, alternate animation and repose in the delivery, as well as a sober and appropriate action, are the indispensable conditions which will enable them to impress their auditors. We would advise singers, in practising, to declaim the words of their songs before singing them. It is said that Voltaire made one of his pupils, who had a tendency towards exuberant gesticulation, recite a piece with her hands tied to her sides. Salvini, vhom I consider the finest speaker I ever heard, is a striking example the impression made by a musical and sonorous voice.

Lloyd states that

> " The player's province they vainly try
> Who want those powers—deportment, voice, and eye."

He also lays down certain elocutionary laws, which, quaint and amusing as they are, are worthy of reproduction :—

> " 'Tis not enough the voice be sound and clear,
> 'Tis modulation that must charm the ear ;
> The voice all modes of passion can express
> That marks the proper word with proper stress,
> But none emphatic can that actor call
> Who lays an equal emphasis on all.
> Some o'er the tongue the laboured measures roll,
> Slow and deliberate, as the parting toll,
> Point every stop, mark every pause, so long
> Their words like stage processions stalk along ;
> Till affectation but creates disgust
> And e'en in speaking we may deem to just.
> In vain for them the pleasing measure flows,
> Whose recitation runs it all to prose ;
> Repeating what the poet sets not down,
> The verb disjoining from its friendly noun,
> While pause and break and repetition join
> To make a discord in each tuneful line.
> Some placid natures fill the allotted scene
> With lifeless drone, insipid and serene ;
> While others thunder every couplet o'er,
> And almost crack your ears with rent and roar.
> More nature oft, and finest strokes, are shown
> In the low whisper than tempestuous tone ;
> And Hamlet's hollow voice and fixed amaze
> More powerful terror to the mind conveys,
> Than he who, swollen with big impetuous rage,
> Bullies the bulky phantom off the stage."
>              &c.,        &c.

— R. LLOYD.

# CHAPTER I.

## THE VOICE.

THE human voice, through the influence of age, sex, and constitution, undergoes many modifications. Besides the striking difference existing between the voices of various human beings, there are many qualities or shades belonging to the voice of the same individual. Every voice is capable of assuming the inflexions caused by the different passions, and of imitating animals, as well as nearly all the noises which strike the ear.

The manner of taking breath being the first consideration in the formation of the voice, we will consider the functions of the organs employed in respiration.

The mechanism employed in speaking, as well as in singing, is the combined action of four sets of organs, which, though they act simultaneously, have each their peculiar and independent functions, namely :—

| | | | |
|---|---|---|---|
| I. The lungs, | - | - | The bellows or air supply. |
| II. The larynx, | - | - | Vibratory organs. |
| III. The pharynx, | - | - | Reflecting organs. |
| IV. Organs of the mouth, | | - | The articulating organs. |

This and the following chapter are chiefly based on Manuel Garcia's "Treatise on Singing," published by Messrs Hutchings & Romer.

## THE LUNGS (THE BELLOWS, OR AIR CHEST).

The lungs are the indispensable agents for respiration, and are placed below the organ of the voice, performing functions analogous to the bellows of a church organ ; that is to say, they furnish the wind required for producing the different sonorous vibrations. Air enters into and escapes from the lungs by a multitude of minute tubes, called the *bronchial* tubes, which, as they ascend to the throat, unite into a single highly elastic pipe, known by anatomists as the *trachea*. This, rising vertically up the anterior part of the neck, communicates with the larynx, the organ next in succession. The lungs are a receptacle for the accumulation of air, and do not, as most persons suppose, give origin to the sounds commonly denominated *chest notes*. The cause of this error is as follows :— Men—not women—experience in singing or speaking, in the lower tones of their voice, a strong vibration, both in the chest and the back, but (analogously in this respect to the harmonic board of pianos and violins) the chest receives the vibrations only by transmission, having no power to originate them. These organs are enclosed by the ribs, and rest upon the diaphragm, which wholly separates them from the abdomen. The development of the lungs in the act of inspiration may be affected simultaneously from above, downwards, by the contraction of the diaphragm, and laterally by the distention of the ribs. Whether these two operations could be performed independently of each other is at least doubtful, but perfect inspiration appears to depend upon their united action. With females, indeed, the act of inspiration is more usually effected by the raising of the chest ; but it may be very much questioned whether this is not mainly due to the confinement in which their ribs are habitually held.

## MECHANICAL ACTION IN BREATHING.

### (THE BREATH.)

No persons become accomplished speakers or singers until ~y possess an entire control over the breath—the very element of sound. In order that the lungs may freely receive the external air, the chest must be sufficiently capacious to allow of their full dilation ; and in effecting this, the diaphragm, which is a wide covered muscle separating the lungs from the cavity of the abdomen, plays an important part. The action of breathing consists of two separate operations, the first being that of inspiration, by which the lungs draw in the external air ; and the second, that of expiration, by which they give out the air just inspired. To insure easy inspiration, it is requisite that the head be erect, the shoulders thrown back without stiffness, and the chest expanded. This double movement enlarges the compass or the circumference of the lungs ; first at their base, and subsequently throughout their whole extent, leaving them full liberty to expand, until they are completely filled with air.

When the lungs have been *gradually* filled, without any *jerking* movement, they have the power of retaining the air without effort ; this *slow* and complete inspiration is what the Italians call *respiro*, as contrasted with that slight and hurried inspiration which gives the lungs that slight supply, merely sufficient for a movement, and technically termed the *mezzo respiro*. In neither case, however, should the passage of the air through the glottis be attended by any noise, as besides being offensive to the ear, it would make the throat both dry and stiff.

Of course the mechanical art of expiration is precisely the reverse of inspiration, consisting simply in effecting a gentle gradual pressure of the throat and diaphragm on the lungs when charged with air ; for if the movements of the ribs and of the diaphragm were to take place suddenly, they would cause the air to escape all at once.

We would remark, that by submitting the lungs to a particular exercise, their power and elasticity will greatly increase. This exercise consists of four distinct and successive practical operations now to be described :—

> *Firstly.*—The pupil should gently and slowly inhale, for a few seconds, as much air as the chest can well contain.

*Secondly.*—After taking a deep breath the air must be exhaled again very gently and slowly.

*Thirdly.*—Fill the lungs and keep them inflated for the longest possible time.

*Fourthly.*—Exhale completely, and leave the chest empty as long as the physical powers will conveniently allow. It must be confessed, that all these exercises are at first very exhausting, and must be separately practised.

After long intervals of rest, however, the two first, namely, the gentle inspirations and expirations, will be more equally effected by nearly closing the mouth in such a way as to leave only a very slight aperture for the passage of air. By these means the pupil will acquire steadiness of voice. The breath influences the speaking voice as well as the mode or character of vocal execution, being capable of rendering it either steady or vacillating, connected or unconnected, powerful or feeble, expressive or the reverse.

## FORMATION OF SOUND.

### (THE LARYNX, OR SECOND APPARATUS.)

The larynx, which is immediately dependent on the respiratory apparatus, forms the registers, the different degrees of brightness and dulness of sounds, and the volume and intensity of the voice.

It is the generator of the voice, and forms the protuberance in the front of the throat, perceptible alike to sight and touch, more developed in the male subject, and usually called "Adam's apple." In the centre of the larynx a narrow passage exists, formed by two tendons stretching horizontally across it, one on the right side, the other on the left. These are called vocal *ligaments*, and the opening between them is called the glottis (whence they are often called the *lips* of the glottis). And to these ligaments, or lips, alone are we indebted for the vibration of the voice.

Modern science has rendered it possible for all who desire it, make an inspection of the vocal ligaments while in action in their larynx. Most doctors use the instrument known as Garcia's laryngoscope for the treatment of throat diseases. In this way a practical illustration of this matter can be obtained with little difficulty.

The mechanical action of the voice is solely formed by periodical compressions and expansions of air during its exit from the glottis. The two small lips in the larynx, which combine to form the glottis or passage for the breath, come into contact with each other, causing below them an accumulation of air, which, owing to the pressure it then undergoes, acquires elasticity, and escapes with sudden expansion through the opening of the glottis. The alternate contractions and dilations, causing successive and regular expansions of air, give origin to the voice. Perhaps the best idea the reader can form of this action is from the vibration of the lips when pressed to the mouth-piece of a trumpet in the act of producing a sound. On the rapidity with which the glottis opens and closes depends the higher or lower sound. It is to be remarked, moreover, that the quickness of the alterations increases inversely to the length of the vibratory orifice. Experience proves that every variety of sound, including, not only the singing voice throughout its whole extent, but the *speaking* voice, and even the *shriek*, is the result of a few primitive and fundamental laws, and may be classified according to register, vibratory quality, and intensity.

## THE REGISTERS.

We mean by register, a series of homogeneous sounds resulting from the use of the same mechanism.

The registers are as follows :—

THE CHEST VOICE (*voce di petto*).
THE FALSETTO VOICE (*falsetto*).
THE HEAD VOICE (*voce di testa*).

## FORMATION OF REGISTERS IN FEMALE VOICES.
### CHEST NOTES.

The chest voice has much greater power of vibration than the falsetto, and requires accordingly a more energetic action of the glottis. This action is most easily called into play by the pronunciation of the Italian *i* or English *e*. The compass of this register, physiologically, may be included in all ladies' voices between E flat below the lines and B or even C third space. In the application, singers must pass from the chest to the falsetto note, between E flat first line and F first space.

### FALSETTO.

The falsetto, a term which is commonly applied to the medium of the voice, is generally more veiled than the head or chest voice, and requires a greater expenditure of air. It extends between D below the lines and C third space. The names of chest, falsetto, and head voice are erroneous, although they are commonly used.

### THE HEAD REGISTER.

The head notes have more brilliancy than the falsetto register, and are obtained by a firm pressure of the lips of the glottis against each other. The head voice extends from C sharp third space to the highest notes of the soprano.

### INTENSITY AND VOLUME OF VOICE.

Intensity of sounds depends on the quantity of air used in producing a pure vibration. The glottis should close entirely after each vibration; because if constantly open, the waste of breath would, beyond all doubt, produce *weak* instead of strong notes. The glottis must, therefore, be constricted in proportion to the pressure given to the air. Volume of sound depends on the cavity formed above the glottis.*

* For further particulars see M. Garcia's "School of Singing," chapter "Classification of Cultivated Voices."

## ON THE EMISSION AND THE QUALITIES OF THE VOICE.

A good, sustained, and resonant quality of the voice being the first desideratum for singers, actors, and public speakers, it is necessary to correct the faults to which all uncultivated voices are liable. Some voices, for instance, are tremulous ; others nasal, guttural, veiled, harsh, shrieking, &c. ; while many are deficient in power, compass, steadiness, elasticity, and mellowness. To correct or obviate the above-mentioned faults, we must study the organ which modifies the sound and produces the various qualities of the voice, namely, the pharynx.

## THE PHARYNX, OR REFLECTING ORGANS.

The pharynx is an elastic cavity visible at the back of the mouth. It is limited by the back wall of the throat and the front arch of the palate. It modifies the sound and produces the various qualities of the voice, which, in leaving the tongue, is echoed and reflected by it. The moment a sound is emitted, it becomes subject to the influence of the vocal tube through which it passes, which tube, having the power of lengthening or shorten-ing, contracting or expanding, and of changing its curvilinear form to that of a right angle, most perfectly fulfils the functions of a reflector to the voice ; thence the variety of " timbre " or resonant quality will correspond to the multitudinous mechanical changes of which the vocal tube is susceptible. By *timbre* is meant the peculiar, and, in fact, variable character that can be assured by each register, even in the formation of the vowels.

We shall understand the movements of the pharynx if we consider it as a deep and highly elastic pipe, beginning below at the larynx, forming a curve at the arch of the soft palate and ending above at the mouth ; a tube which, when at its shortest dimensions, forms only a slight curve, and at its longest nearly a right angle. The larynx in the former case rises towards the soft palate, and the latter dropping to meet it ; whereas in the latter case, the larynx drops and the soft palate rises—thus making the distance between them greater. The Italian vowels *i* and *e* would cause the former of these two functions of the larynx and soft palate, whilst the Italian vowels *o* and *u* would cause the latter action. Laughing has the same effect as the *i* and *e*; yawning, on the contrary, that of the vowel *u*. In conclusion, the short and gently curved shape produces the bright timbre, while the sombre is caused by the lengthened and strongly curved form. These two "timbres," open and close, or bright or dull, are the leading qualities of the voice. This close relationship between the different vowel sounds and the various forms assumed by the pharynx constitute a subject which will be especially considered when we speak of the fourth set of organs—those of the mouth, in treating of articulation.

## TIMBRES.

Every change of timbre, of which all sounds are susceptible, originates in a corresponding change of the tube of the pharynx; and as this flexible tube is capable of undergoing countless varieties of form, it follows that the modifications of all sounds are also numberless. The *ear can always detect* by the quality of a sound the shape assumed by the tube. Among all these shades and changes, those are to be selected which in all respects best suit the voice of the student. That sound is especially to be preferred, which is round, ringing, and mellow.

To obtain this brightness and roundness in the sound, the pupil should draw breath slowly, and then produce the sound by a neat resolute articulation or *stroke* of the *glottis* upon the broad Italian vowel *a*. If this movement be properly executed the sound will come out bright and round. Care, however, must be taken to *pitch* the sound at once on the note itself and *not to slur up* to it, or feel the way to it.

The pupil must also be warned against the confounding the articulation or stroke of the glottis with the stroke of the chest, which latter resembles the act of coughing, or the effort made in ...ing some obstruction from the throat. This stroke or act of coughing out the notes of the chest causes a great loss of breath, rendering the sounds aspirated, stifled, and uncertain in tone. The function of the chest is solely to supply air not to *throw* it out violently.

The glottis is prepared for articulation by closing it, which causes a momentary accumulation of air below, and it is then opened by a sudden and vigorous stroke—similar to the action of the lips when strongly emphasising the letter *p*.

Actors as well as singers may be recommended to practise this action of the glottis on the seven Italian vowels, *a, è, è, i, o, ò, u*, and also in all the notes forming the compass of their voice, a clear and sonorous tone of voice being the first desideratum for the one as well as for the other.

There are several defects calculated to injure the beauty of the voice. The most common of these we shall at once point out, and at the same time show the best means to correct them.

## GUTTURAL TIMBRE.

Whenever the tongue rises or swells at its base, it drives back the epiglottis—a little cap or valve, that covers the air pipe and causes the food to pass directly into the gullet or swallowing pipe —on the columns of ascending air, and causes the voice to be emitted with a *guttural*, choked sound. This position of the tongue may be ascertained by outwardly pressing the top of the larynx with the finger, whilst in the act of singing. The best method of correcting this defective timbre will at once be inferred.

Should the glottis be raised over the finger, it indicates that the tongue becomes convex at the root. Should the glottis remain under the finger, it indicates that the tongue remains passive at the root. It should lie at the bottom of the mouth, forming a hollow. In the act of yawning, the glottis is lowered, the soft palate raised, and the throat in general is relaxed entirely. Thus no contraction being possible, the voice loses its choky and guttural sound.

The tongue is the chief agent employed in transforming sounds into vowels, which should be done principally by the movements of its edges, while its *base* should always remain passive. It may be added, that the separation of the jaws should be nearly uniform for all vowels.

## NASAL TIMBRE.

When the soft palate is too much relaxed, the voice will probably acquire a nasal character, for the column of vocal air is reflected or echoed immediately in the nasal fossæ or cavities before being emitted by the mouth. On *pinching* the *nostrils* we may perceive whether the column of air on leaving the larynx is directed against the nassal fossæ before entering the mouth, or whether it passes immediately through this latter cavity. The way to correct this fault is simply to raise the soft palate by inhaling deeply, with the mouth well opened.

## CAVERNOUS OR HOLLOW SOUNDING TIMBRE.

The voice will become dull and cavernous if any obstacle be offered to the progress of the waves of sound. The rising of the tongue at its tip is alone sufficient to produce this effect. The swelling of the tonsils may also present another obstacle, and give the voice a muffled character. This swelling, to which young persons are liable, constitutes a difficulty in forming the head voice and extending its compass.

## VEILED SOUNDS.

Of all the qualities of voice the most objectionable is that which is open, and yet has no brilliancy. Be it remembered, however, that the veiled quality of the voice may be corrected by constricting or contracting the glottis, which will be best y pronouncing the English vowel *e*.

## SOUND OBTAINED BY INSPIRATION.

Sound can be formed not only when the air is expelled from the chest, but also when it passes through the larynx to enter the lungs. This voice is gruff and uneven. It is exclusively used in declamatory passages, where the actor resorts to suppressed sobbing or struggling for breath to express intense passion, or in death scenes. Great caution and taste must dictate the use of such resources. Where it is judiciously employed, it greatly adds to the general effect, whereas it would be entirely out of place if it were applied to the expression of ordinary sentiments.

# CHAPTER II.

## ON ARTICULATION.

NEATNESS of articulation in speaking or singing is of the first importance. A singer or public speaker who is not distinctly understood wearies his auditors, and destroys almost all the effect of the music or of the sentiments he has to express, by obliging the hearers to make continual efforts to catch the sense of the words.

Where the singer or public speaker has not attentively analysed the mechanism that produces both vowels and consonants, his articulation will be deficient in ease and energy, inasmuch as he has not learned the secret of giving that development and equilibrium to the voice which he might attain in simple vocalisation, and cannot employ at pleasure the timbre suitable to the passion he wishes to express. Often actors have not sufficient ear to enable them to study singing ; yet I would strongly recommend them to make themselves thoroughly acquainted with the mechanical actions of the larynx, as explained in the preceding chapter, as well as with the mechanism that produces both vowels and consonants, to be treated of in this chapter. In the first instance they will acquire that vibrating, sonorous quality so impressive in declamation, obtaining at the same time such perfect control over their voice as will enable them to modulate at pleasure, without straining it, until huskiness and coarseness of tone have taken the place of musical sounds, whether soft or energetic.

Our remarks on this subject will be comprised under the following heads :—

> VOWELS.
> CONSONANTS.
> THE QUANTITY OF VOWELS.
> THE QUANTITY OF CONSONANTS.

## ON VOWELS.

The voice, both in speaking and in singing, is produced by precisely the same set of organs, and both the speaking and the singing voice issue from the same cavities, namely—the mouth and nostrils. Of these the mouth is the more important, as its sides and internal organs are the principal agents of articu-lation. In fact the tongue, palate, teeth and lips, all con-tribute in turn to the modification of the different elements of speech. These are aided by the jaws, which, by their ever-varying play, have no inconsiderable share in the quality of the sounds produced. Thus, the mouth, owing to its capa-bility for contraction or expansion, can, by the modification of its diameter, length, and internal form, give to the voice in its exit a correspondingly different sound. The vowels are the result of those modifications which sounds receive in passing through the vocal tube. The simplest sound emitted therefrom represents to our ear the condition of the pipe while air is being forced through it ; and all the differences in simple sounds indicate cor-responding differences in its form. The Italians usually recognise only seven vowels—*a è è i o ò u*. Nevertheless, there should be at least nine vowel sounds ; for in the high notes of each register, the French vowels *e* and *u* are absolutely indispensable. The practice of languages proves that the number of vowels, and shades of vowels, is unlimited ; for though writing represents

vowels by means of invariable signs, there is a marked difference
in the sound of each when uttered by different individuals.
Moreover, a person pronouncing any word does not always give
to the vowels it contains the same stress and sound; for so soon
as any passion animates a speaker, the vowels unavoidably receive
its influence, and strike our ear by the clearness or dulness of
their shadings, and the brilliancy or the sombre quality of their
*timbre*.  In the word "anima," for instance, the *a* will not maintain the same sonorousness in a passage of tenderness, as in one
of anger, raillery, entreaty, or menace.

On comparing these remarks with those previously made on
the *timbres*, the reader will observe a close resemblance between
this mechanism and that of vowels, whereby they mutually depend
on one another; indeed one cannot be altered without changing
the other.  This observation is most important in its results, for
it will enable the singer to determine what timbre for each vowel
is best suited to the proposed effect, and at the same time to
maintain a perfect equality throughout his voice.  Indeed, the
choice of *timbre* for each vowel is dependent on two different
things, the verbal or declamatory accent, and evenness of voice.
A few examples will illustrate this.

The timbre should vary with every varying passion to be expressed.  For instance, if the melody and words indicate deep
grief, a bright quality would evidently make the voice belie the
sentiment.

The brilliant tone which would suit the following words, in
Moore's charming song, "The Young May Moon":—

> "Then, awake! the heavens look bright, my dear,
> 'Tis never too late for delight, my dear,"—

would appear absurdly jocund, and therefore out of place, in the
following lines of the old poet Chaucer in the words he puts
into the mouth of the dying Arcite:—

> Alas, the death! alas mine Emelie,
> Alas, departing of our company!
> —(*Arcite's dying address.*)

On the other hand, if the sentiment to be expressed is that of *gaiety* and animation, or if melody breathes the same, a clear timbre can alone communicate appropriate brilliancy to the voice. In such a case, dull or covered *timbre* would produce a hoarse effect.

But, in order to obtain evenness of voice, the student should by clever management modify a vowel, insensibly sounding it as the voice ascends, and brightening it as it descends ; by this means a seeming equality results from a real, but well-concealed inequality of the vocal sounds. This precept applies to each register throughout the entire compass. If a vowel remained constantly open, as the *a* when sounded in the word "father," it would give brightness to the low and middle sounds, while high notes would be shrill and shrieking ; whereas a vowel that is invariably covered, like the *o* in the word "monte," would give richness to the high notes, and make low ones veiled and dull.

This method applied to all vowels will supply us with the following principles :—

The *a* approaches the open *o*.
The open *è* approaches the *é ;* and next to it, the *eu*.
The *i* (Italian) approaches the *u*, without the aid of the lips.
The *o* approaches the *ou*.

When a vowel is to be brightened, an exactly opposite process to that above indicated is requisite,—the *ou* approaches *o ; o, a ;* and so on with the rest. Vowels which are very acute—as *i* (Italian) and *u* (French),—if sung as they are spoken, would contract the voice and inconvenience it. To avoid this, a pupil should open these vowels a little more than is required for spoken pronunciation. Our experience proves the following exercises to be most useful in assisting pupils to master all the inflections of voice which render singing effective.

Produce a note in a single breath ; pass gradually through all the *timbres*, from the brightest to the most sombre ; and then, in another breath, reverse the exercise, by going from the sombre : each note should be given with uniform power throughout. The real efficacy of this exercise, however, is confined to the chest register, and between the notes *la*, and *fa* ♯, ; assisted by the exercise for uniting the registers, it will enable a pupil to master all the movements of the throat, and to produce at will sounds of every description.

It has been observed that the voice is emitted by two channels; the second of which is the nose, whose function is to render the voice more sonorous when the mouth is open, and entirely to change sounds, by giving them a nasal tone when the latter is closed, either by the tongue in pronouncing the letter *n*, or by the lips in sounding *m*. Italians have no nasal vowels, properly so called; for with them the nasal echo on *n* or *m* only takes place when one of these two consonants begins or ends the syllable, never blending with the vowel sound; as, for example, *A . . . . ngelo, Te . . . . mpo.* To conclude, *vowels should always be attacked by the stroke of the glottis, and with power suitable to the phrase.* Pupils, however, must scrupulously avoid preceding these with an *h*, or aspiration, for the use of this latter must be confined to sighs, &c.; its employment under any other circumstances only alienates the sense of words, or induces faults.*

### OF CONSONANTS.

Consonants are produced by two different operations of the articulatory organs :—First—By pressure of two parts of the instrument against each other, and the explosion of air heard at the moment of their separation. Secondly—From the incomplete and variable meeting of these same organs, and the different and continuous sounds emitted by the air so confined. It is from these two processes that we derive the classification of consonants into explosive and sustained—a division of the first importance in the art of singing and speaking.

---

* A very common fault with pupils is to stiffen the elevator-muscles of the jaw. A plan for curing this, is to place sideways, between the upper and lower teeth, a small piece of wood or cork ; likewise a riband may be passed over the chin, immediately below the lower lip, and tied at the back of the neck. This done, every vowel should be successively practised, with as little effort as possible.

## EXPLOSIVE CONSONANTS.

It is the distinctive character of these consonants to make no noise prior to the explosion which gives them utterance. In forming them, the organs are first closed, and again separated, when the consonant is immediately heard. These two opposite and indispensable movements are called respectively—the preparation and explosion of a consonant ; and it is by this process that the letters *p*, *f*, *t*, *c* (Italian *cio*), and *k*, are enunciated. During preparation, the air is intercepted and collected ; and the explosion that follows is proportioned to the degree of preparation and amount of air collected to produce it ; an effect much resembling that of the stroke of the glottis in attacking simple sounds. *b*, *d*, and *g* hard, also, are reckoned among the explosive consonants ; only the explosion is preceded by a slight noise lasting while the mouth or pharynx is filling with air,—the former cavity for *b* and *d*, the latter for *g*.

## SUSTAINED CONSONANTS.

These consonants produce a whistling sound, that may be prolonged at pleasure, such as *ch*, *x*, and *s* ; or else they are given out with a continuous noise, like *m*, *n*, *gn*, *l*, and *gl*. The first of these arises from a partial closing of the organs in various ways, which we shall not attempt to describe ; the second is accomplished by their *perfect contact*. The noise thus emitted may be easily converted into a musical sound ; a transformation which enables a voice to be sustained from one syllable to another,—a result giving a much increased breadth of style. Two articulatory organs always act in combination, and in five principal ways, thus :—

The lips act together in pronouncing *p* and *m*.

The upper teeth with the lower lip, as in *f* and *v*.

The end of the tongue with the teeth, as in *t* and *d*.

The front part of the tongue with the palate, as in *n* and *l*.

The base of the tongue with the palatine arch, as in *k* and *g* hard.

Each of the combinations above enumerated, gives rise to a

B

different class of consonants, and these combined, form the total of the consonants in use.

In the following table, the consonants have been divided, according to our view of the subject, into five different classes, grouped according to the names of the organs engaged in producing them, and to their explosive or sustained character, with the successive organic operations :— .

| | | |
|---|---|---|
| **CLASS I.** Labials. | Explosive P (pure) ... ... | Complete closing,—silent preparation,—explosion. |
| | Explosive B (mixed)... ... | Complete closing,—slight preparatory sound,—explosion. |
| | Sustained M ... ... ... | Complete closing,—sustained nasal sound,—explosion. |
| **CLASS II.** Labio-dentals. | Explosive F (pure) ... ... | Complete closing,—silent preparation,—explosion. |
| | | F may be classed either among explosive or sustained sounds, according to the energy displayed in its articulation. The first effect, which is also the boldest, helps to complete the classification. |
| | Sustained V ... ... ... | Incomplete closing,—silent preparation,—explosion. |
| | | V may be, according to the will of him who articulates it, either a mixed explosive, or sustained sound. The second of these is preferable. |
| **CLASS III.** Linguo-dentals. | Explosive T (pure) .... ... | Complete closing,—silent preparation,—explosion. |
| | Explosive D (mixed)... ... | Complete closing,—slight preparatory sound,—explosion. |
| | Sustained TH (as in English *the*), the Spanish C (as in *cena*), Z | Incomplete closing, — sustained whistling. |
| **CLASS IV.** Linguo-palatals. | Explosive pure C (Italian *cio*) | Complete closing,—silent preparation,—explosion. |
| | Sustained L, GL, N, GN... | Incomplete closing, — sustained sounds. |
| | Sustained R ... ... ... | Sustained vibration of the tip of the tongue. |
| | Sustained French J, CH, X, hard S, soft S ... ... | Incomplete closing,—whistlings of different kinds. |

| | | | |
|---|---|---|---|
| **CLASS V.**<br>**Linguo-**<br>**gutturals.** | Explosive (pure) C hard,<br>K, Q  ... ... ... ... | Complete closing, —silent prepara-<br>tion,—explosion. |
| | Explosive (mixed) G hard... | Complete closing, —slight prepara-<br>tory sound, —explosion. |
| | Incomplete closing  ...  ... | Sustained sound, effected by the<br>vibration of the uvula. |

## SUMMARY.

5 pure explosives : P, F, T, Italian C, hard C, K, Q : Silent preparation,—explosion.

3 mixed      „      B, D, hard G.—Slight preparatory sound,—
explosion.

5 sustained  „      L, GL, M, N, GN.

Various noises or continued whistlings.—C, H, R, S hard, S
soft, X, Z, TH, V, &c.

Pupils should pay especial attention to the point at which the
organs come in contact, and the process which aids them in forming each consonant. It is from neglecting to give this subject
due attention, that some singers or actors add to the movements
required others which are quite useless ; for instance—putting the
lips and jaw into action when the tongue alone should be occupied. Others, again, languidly drag the organs from one consonant to another, and allow the echoing of a vowel, thus :—

> Ise thisse a daggere thate I see before me,
> The handle towardsse my hanncde ?
> Comme lette me clutche thee,
> I have thee notte, and yette I see thee stille.

MACBETH.

## ON ACCENTS.

The human voice exhibits the four following features :—

I. The variable duration of the sounds.

II. Their *timbre.*

III. Their rise or fall in the gamut.

IV. Their different degrees of intensity.

In each language it is easy to discern different kinds of
accents ; as, for instance—the grammatical accent, written accent,

logical or verbal accent, accent of sentiment, and, lastly, the national accent. We shall confine ourselves to the consideration of the grammatical and sentimental accents, as they alone are connected with our subject.

## ON QUANTITY (*Accento tonico*).

In speaking, a person, led on by rapidity of thought, stops only at a single point of each word, on the most emphatic syllable,—that, in fact, on which the action of the organs is principally displayed. A strong accent which determines the importance of the emphatic syllable, constitutes what is termed *prosody*. It is marked, in almost all languages, on one syllable only, in each word, however long that word may be; and is simply caused by prolonging the time occupied in uttering it. A little attention will soon enable a student to discover the accented portion in a word; for example :—

> Underneath *this stone* doth *lie*,
> As much *beau*ty as could *die* ;
> Which in *life* did *har*bour give,
> To more *vir*tue than doth *live*,—
> If at *all* she had a *fault*,
> Leave it *bur*ied in *this vault*.
>
> EPITAPH ON A LADY, (Ben Jonson).

All words have an accent—even monosyllables; and this accent varies with the expression of our feelings, the most important word in a phrase always receiving the strongest emphasis.

## EMPHASIS ON CONSONANTS.

Besides prosodaical accents, a student should consider the stress to be laid on certain consonants ; for example :—

*m*        *tt*

Temple, netting.

This emphasis answers to prolongation of vowels. We will now state under what circumstances consonants should be forcibly pronounced. *Firstly*, In order to surmount any mechanical difficulty of articulation ; *secondly*, To give strength to the expression of

some sentiment; *thirdly,* To render words audible in large buildings. Expression depends greatly on the weight and strength given
to articulation.   *Consonants express the force of a sentiment, just as
vowels express its nature.*   We are always impressed by words
strongly accentuated, because they appear to be dictated by some
acute passion ; and of course the most important word should
receive the strongest emphasis ; for example :—

> The *m*ind that *b*roods o'er *g*uilty *w*oes
> Is like the *s*corpion *g*irt by *f*ire.
>
> "REMORSE" (Lord Byron).

These consonants, thus marked, add great effect to the phrase.
The attack of vowels by a stroke of the glottis is alone equally
efficacious ; but, in many passages, it would be quite misplaced.
The necessity for being understood generally causes a speaker
to lay a stress upon consonants, in proportion to the size of a
building ; hence, emphasis is made stronger in declamation than
in speaking, and still more so in song.   The last consonant in
every syllable ought to be expressed with as much precision as the
initiatory one.   Negligence in this respect is the chief cause of
indistinctness and incorrectness of articulation in singing as in
speaking ; for example :—

> How clea*r*, how kee*n*, how marvellously brigh*t*
> The effluence fro*m* yo*n* mountain'*s* distan*t* be*d*,
> Whic*h* strow*n* wi*th* *s*now as smoo*th* as heav*en* ca*n* she*d*,
> Shines like another su*n* o*n* morta*l* sigh*t*,
> Uprisen *as* if to chec*k* approaching nigh*t*,
> An*d* all he*r* twinkli*ng* star*s*.
>
> "THE MOUNTAIN TOP," Nov. 1st, 1815 (W. Wordsworth).

## FULNESS AND STEADINESS OF VOICE IN
## PRONOUNCING WORDS.

In singing or speaking, if a singer or actor is unable to render
the emission of his voice independent of the articulation of consonants, the organ receives a certain shock, which destroys all

roundness, firmness, and connection of sounds. To obviate this inconvenience, it is requisite to distinguish the functions and mode of action peculiar to each of the four sets of organs in the vocal apparatus, and that each should perform its respective functions without interfering with any others; for where one organ performs its duties imperfectly,—if the chest should slacken the emission of air,—if the glottis be wanting in power, if the flow of voice be interrupted or weakened after each sentence; if the pharynx form timbres inappropriate to the sentiment,—or if the organs of articulation, incongruously blended, lack the clearness and precision desirable, a singer is said to want method, and an actor to be a bad speaker.

To conclude, we may say that the enunciation of words should be blended with the voice, so that there should be an uninterrupted flow of musical sound especially where eloquent persuasion, or tenderness, have to be expressed. We have still to point out another great fault, and that is a laughable break in the voice (*scrocchi di voce*). Actors, public speakers, as well as singers, must guard against this ridiculous noise. If during the articulation of certain consonants, or the vocalisation of certain passages on high notes, a pupil should neglect to sustain his breath with great resolution, the glottis being naturally obliged to contract its dimensions to produce high notes, will completely close, and stop the voice, re-opening with a ridiculous explosion the instant afterwards.

## PHRASEOLOGY.

Diction, or the art of phrasing, requires besides all the physical qualities and acquirements already stated, a thorough intelligence in the treatment of the sentiments that are to be expressed.

The following rules must necessarily be observed :—

     I. Accent every word slightly.

     II. Cause the principal sentiment of a speech to predominate.

III. Mark every particular sentiment in every phrase by putting proper emphasis on the words ; observe appropriate pauses so as to have repose in the diction, thus avoiding precipitation and confusion ; take breath in the proper places (a point which is often totally disregarded by singers) ; avoid a monotonous prosody or rhythm in the general movement of a phrase. not beginning each phrase loudly and ending it softly.

In subsequent chapters on the analysis of different scenes, we will give a quotation with analytic explanations, combining diction and action.

# CHAPTER III.

## RULES TO BE OBSERVED IN THE CONCERT-ROOM.

WHEN the artiste appears before the public, his general appearance should be such as to excite interest. He must ascend the platform deliberately, not running up the steps, and proceed at once to the place he intends occupying; keeping his head upright, without stiffness or affectation. Should anything be in his way as he walks to his place, let him wait until it is removed, as too much precipitation would cause confusion, or betray nervous excitement. Having reached his place on the platform, the artiste will stand erect facing the public and looking straight before him; his body firmly balanced on the feet, heel to heel, without awkwardness or stiffness, and the knees straightened; the general appearance indicative of self-possession and confidence. Let him carefully avoid looking round to acknowledge his friends by glance or gesture. Such an act of familiarity would not only be taken for an excess of confidence, but would divert his mind from his work. Having assumed his position, his next action will be to acknowledge, with a bow, the reception given to him by the public.

In the salutation to the public, anything like an appearance of servility should be avoided. It is an act of courtesy, not a request for indulgence, or for favourable criticism. On the other hand, any expression of familiarity, such as is sometimes seen on the part of popular favourites, in gestures of the hand (placing it on the heart or waving it) is awkward and vulgar ; the hands should hang quietly by the sides.

Care must be taken not to stick the elbows out, as is often done, or to bow too much from the waist, as the result would be more grotesque than graceful. In fact, a slow and gentle inclination of the head and shoulders is quite sufficient.

When the bow has been made the head and shoulders are raised, and the eyes are again directed forward.

FIG. 1.

The curtsy is the proper salutation for the lady to make on appearing on the platform. Above all, it should be quiet and graceful, and not too low. Kissing of hands, in acknowledgment of applause, is to be deprecated.

When seated before the public, great attention must be paid to the following rules. *Never* cross the legs : as it is an attitude of a familiar and careless appearance. The knees must not be far apart, as it would cause the toes to be turned inwards ; this again would be a very awkward position. The correct way of sitting is with one foot slightly more forward than the other (Fig. 1), the hands holding the music, the arms close to the body : the body itself leaning well back in the chair, so as to present an erect and dignified, although at the same time an

unassuming position.    The act of sitting down and getting up
must be performed *slowly* and with care, so as not to betray
nervousness, or, on the other hand, to cause a painful impression
by a careless or vulgar movement, or demeanour, such as is shown
in Figs. 2 and 3.

The expression of the face must be pleasant, and betray neither

FIG. 2.

fear nor anxiety, as the effect would be painful for those who have
come to *see* as well as hear.    In the act of singing the mouth must
not be opened too widely, but simply the width of the first finger ;
nor yet contracted at the sides, so as not to disfigure the usual

expression of the face.    The eyebrows must not be lifted up.    In
breathing, great care must be taken not to lift the shoulders.

Fig. 3.

# CHAPTER IV.

---

## GENERAL OBSERVATIONS ON ACTING.

*(Vera ars est artem celare.)*

TO act, from the Latin *agere*, does not mean to throw one's self into all sorts of attitudes, or to discard nature, in order to submit to theatrical conventionalities. It simply means, to make movements, or action. In speaking, we give force to our words by appropriate motions of the body and limbs, as well as by the expression of the face. In so doing we simply follow the *impulse of nature*. Therefore, *to be natural* is the first consideration for an actor. We differ in our movements according to our temperament and to our nationalities. Every nation—and in some cases we might even say each separate great division of a nation—has its typical actions, movements, expressions, as it has its separate dialects. The pantomimic action of a Neapolitan differs totally from that of a Lombard. The actor, whose calling it is to impersonate different characters, as well as different nationalities, will have to study and observe human nature in order to become thoroughly acquainted with others' characters and imitate their gestures with perfect ease ; in fact, to assimilate his own nature to theirs. This is *the true art* which always proves irresistible. In order to obtain this result it is necessary that the actor should restrict himself as far as possible to the parts which best suit his *physical qualifications.* Otherwise he will be obliged to resort to conventional means which the traditions left by other actors will give him, and which will be in many cases unsuited to his own nature. Thus he will fail to impress on others what he does not feel himself. Who would care to see Othello, short, feeble, with a meagre voice? It is necessary that in his appearance the Moor should realise Shakespeare's ideal of the warrior, the man of the camp, who loves the " pomp and circumstance of glorious war." Whatever may be the line of acting an actor chooses, tragedy, melodrama, high or low comedy, he must always idealise his impersonation according to the character he has to represent, and also follow the gradations of nature, which always vary in our passions with more or less intensity. In so doing he will be *natural.* What could be more absurd than Iago playing his part with the voice and manners of Banquo's murderers in Macbeth, although he be a murderer himself. One would wonder at such a man being in such good society. Taking even Banquo's assassins, although men of rough manners, what would be the feeling of the spectator if they were to present themselves before Macbeth in an abject garb, assuming the revolting manners and voice of convicts, addressing him as they would a fellow of their own stamp. Such an interpretation would entirely destroy the effect of a highly-impressive scene—Macbeth himself would not appeal to feelings of outraged honour and revenge in such miscreants. Such low familiarity on their part would little harmonise with the language Shakespeare put into their mouths,—*First Murderer:* " We are men, my liege." *Second Murderer:* " I am one, my liege, whom the vile blows and buffets of the world have so incensed, that I am reckless what I do to spite the world," &c.

Such intense determination does not admit of exuberance of gesticulation nor of a gruff loud tone of voice ; and yet, by inferior actors these are often associated with the parts, because the men are murderers,—a murderer, with them, being necessarily of the " Bill Sykes " type. There are, in fact, several degrees of refinement in the interpretation of a part ; let the actor always choose the higher degree.

The expression of the face, and the outward action by gestures, &c., being the reflex of our sentiments, the " mirror of our soul," modes of acting are infinitely varied. Our aim is to classify each movement of the . face or action of the body according to the sentiments or passion that is to be expressed. We will consider these passions and feelings in different chapters, giving an analysis of their particular treatment. It would be impossible, in anything like the limits of the present volume, to give all the varieties of combined actions, as they are infinite ; we will, therefore, give the fundamental rules for acting, with a general analysis of sentiments and passions.

When once the foundation is laid, let the artiste work upon it according to his own nature.

# CHAPTER V.

## HOW TO WALK THE STAGE.—PRACTICES.

THE method of walking, or what we generally call gait or carriage, is one of the characteristic features which reflect the sentiments of the mind either in its temporary or normal state. The walk of a man of thoughtful, steady mind is regular, although it may by nature be either quick or slow. On the contrary, when the soul is assailed by turbulent or uncertain thoughts of different kinds, the walk becomes unsteady and undecided. Macbeth, whose mind is full of violent passions, has no repose in his movements. His walk is irregular, uncertain; his steps are at times long, at others short; sometimes he will stop suddenly. In one word, his feet cannot carry him too fast when he anticipates the future, nor move too slowly when he considers the past. Othello betrays the agonies of his mind especially in the last scene with Desdemona, when his walk indicates every phase of his torture. The walk is also typical of age, habits, and occupation in life.

Elegance and ease being the first desideratum for actors, we will state in this chapter the general rules to be observed, pointing out at the same time the faults to be avoided, and subdividing each action belonging to the walk into special practices.

I. Cross the stage from the left to the right corner, keeping close to the footlights, the left of the actor as he faces the public being the right of the spectator.

R +-------------------+ L

Suppose the actor standing, in what is called in dancing the second position, on the left-hand corner of the stage, and three-parts turned towards the public, — the right foot being the foremost; the toes slightly turned out, the body erect and well balanced on the left foot; both legs straight, both feet resting firmly on the ground, the arms and hands hanging down naturally without stiffness. In this position, which he will keep throughout the following practices, he will start with the left foot, making his strides rather longer than in the ordinary walk, and walking with a slow and regular step.

The mechanical actions in walking the stage are these:—the foot does not leave the ground suddenly, nor yet does the heel come down first. The toes are the last to leave the ground, and the first to touch it;

FIG. 4.

the body balancing itself gracefully on each leg as the stride is taken ; whilst the knees, slightly bent during each action of the legs, will become straightened, the instant the foot rests on the ground.   As the pupil becomes more at home on the stage, he will lose the conventionality or stiffness that invariably, at first, attends all physical exercises.

On reaching the right-hand corner of the stage, the student must manage so as to finish his walk with the second position, the right foot being the foremost (see Fig. 4).

II. Being in the above attitude he will then turn half round without changing his position, thus finding himself again in the second position, the left foot being foremost.    He will then start on the right foot, and will cross the stage back again to the left-hand corner, observing the same rules as in number one practice.

This and all the following exercises, will have to be repeated until the pupil has acquired perfect ease in all his movements.

III. DESCENDING AND ASCENDING THE STAGE.—Suppose the pupil standing in the second position at the very back of the stage, in the centre and *facing* the public,—he will start, directing his steps to the prompter's box, supposed to be in the centre of the front ; having reached this within a foot, he will find himself in the second position.    Then turning half round, as before, he will walk up the stage taking the same direction, until he has reached the back of the stage.

IV. WALKING A MEASURED DISTANCE.—To walk a measured distance, we must suppose two points ;  one the left-hand corner of the stage, the other a chair placed in the middle of the stage— the left-hand corner near the footlights being the starting-point. The student will first *measure* the exact distance between the two points.    Having done so, he will next calculate the number of steps to be taken.    Before starting he will assume the second position and then advance towards the chair, starting with the left foot first ; on reaching the chair, he must find himself precisely in the second position, with the right foot foremost (see Fig. 4).

V. The student will repeat the above practice, starting from the right-hand corner.    In this instance he will step forward with his right foot first; and, in approaching the chair, will find himself in number two position with the *left* foot foremost.

VI. Rules in Walking Measured Distances.—If we compare Figs. 4 and 5, we see at once the advantage of the position Fig. 4 over Fig. 5, which latter is extremely awkward. This

Fig. 5.

awkwardness can always be avoided by observing the following rule. Suppose a distance of two, four, six, eight, or ten feet, from the left-hand side of the stage to the chair; the pupil, starting with the left foot, will always find himself close to the chair with the *right* foot foremost (Fig. 4).

If the distance between the two points is three, five, seven, nine, or eleven feet, he will have to start with the right foot; although it may be the foremost in the second position. In addition, give the *even* numbers to the left foot, and the odd numbers to the right foot.

We may add, that this second position allows the actor to turn alternately towards a person on the stage, or to the public, scarcely moving his body. The simple fact of turning his heels a few degrees right or left, will suffice to leave him perfect freedom of action, without causing awkward attitudes.

VII. The same practice must be performed from the right-hand side of the stage, giving the even numbers to the right foot, and the odd to the left.

VIII. Interrupted Walks.—Instead of walking a measured distance without pauses or interruptions, let it be done in different stages For instance,—take two steps, and stop; three steps, and stop—four steps, and stop, &c. Combine the number of steps and stoppages according to the distance to be walked; care being taken to fall into the second position at every pause.

IX. Should the walk be interrupted at every step, the position number *one* will have to be assumed; that is heel against heel at every stoppage.* (Fig. 6.)

X. BACKWARD STEPS.—In walking the stage backwards, the student must be careful to balance his body well back at every step, which must be taken slowly, whilst the foot will rest firmly on the ground. Thus he will avoid stumbling or awkwardness in the general attitude. He will stop at every back step, observing the *second* position at every stoppage.

A STAGGERING WALK is frequently resorted to to express different emotions, such as fear, or terror, when the actor staggers back from an object or simply walks away from it without losing sight of it. The above actions can be modified by varying the number of steps in each different stage: for instance, taking either one, two, or three steps before each pause.

XI. COMBINATION OF THE FORWARD AND BACKWARD STEPS. — This walk can be acquired by combining the above practices. Suppose the student

FIG. 6.

* *N.B.*—These practices will have to be repeated in different directions off the stage.

standing in the second position, he will take one, two, or more steps forward ; then stopping, he will turn half round and walk back in the same manner, observing strictly the rules stated on page 33, second practice, page 34, sixth practice.   Having practised this forward and interrupted walk on different parts of the stage, he will repeat the same practice with the backward steps,—that is : he will walk backwards a certain distance, and turning round, will walk once more backwards ; and so again the same distance.

Lastly he will combine the two—for instance, he will walk forward a certain distance, and *without* turning round will walk back again in a backward attitude in the very same direction.   Let it be remembered that at every stoppage he must always find himself in the position shown in Fig. 4, and never in the position shown in Fig. 5.

We would also impress on the student that the toes must never be allowed to turn inwards, either in the action of walking or of turning round.

As the size of the stage varies according to the construction of the theatre, it becomes a necessity for the actor to count the number of steps he has to take.   By doing so he becomes an excellent judge of distances, and knows exactly the spot on which to concentrate the different actions of each scene.   Neglect in this particular often leads to ridiculous positions.   We remember seeing, in Paris, an actress who, being supposed to fall dead in front of the stage, advanced so near the footlights that she had to get up suddenly to avoid the weight of the drop scene, which would have crushed her.

If Valentine, for instance, in his death scene in *Faust*, were to miscalculate the spot on which he has to fall, and staggered back too near the wings, he would crowd the large body of chorus singers into a narrow corner of the stage, thus utterly marring the general effect of the scene.

## CLASSIFICATION OF THE DIFFERENT WALKS.

In music all sentiments are expressed by gradations of sound, otherwise known as light and shade. These gradations are included between the pianissimo and fortissimo. In acting, the light and shade, or the obvious intensity of our sentiments, can be expressed in a similar manner, by the gradations that can be realised between two extreme actions, that is between a short and a long step. For instance, a short or long step taken slowly corresponds to the idea of a gentle or reflective state of mind—quick steps, short or long, to an agitated or energetic temper. As already stated, the walk is typical of the sentiments and passions as well as of the different callings in life. We will, therefore, classify the walks by indicating the kind of steps suitable to the characters to be represented, as well as the actions of the legs.

FIG. 7. (*See next page.*)

Short quick steps are characteristic of young people, whose souls are full of illusion ; whose sentiments are keen, and who are alive to all the sensations that a young mind is ready to receive.——Age and debility will cause old people to take short, tottering steps. The legs in this case will give way at the knee; the feet being lifted up from the ground with some difficulty will cause the toes to drag on the ground.—Stout people generally take short steps, owing to the difficulty they experience in balancing the weighty body on each leg. Old, yet active people often resort to quick short steps.—Persons belonging to the lower stations of life, such as servants, whose calling requires rapidity of movement,—for instance, Suzanna and Figaro in Beaumarchais' *Mariage de Figaro*, will naturally adopt quick, short steps.— For comedy, where the sentiments rarely work up to violent passions, the steps never exceed the stride of ordinary life.—When there is an intention of caricaturing, a long step is often used in farce or comical parts. The incongruity between the stately stride and the commonplace situation always produces a humorous effect. —Bashfulness, or a sense of guilt, will show itself in short, slow steps in the direction of a superior or an accuser.—Short slow steps are typical of submission, gentleness, kindness, modesty, shyness, veneration, reflection. They are associated, as a rule, with quiet or gentle minds.—Long and slow steps betray meditation or great designs, dignity, concentration of thought, pride.—Long and quick steps are indications of strong sentiments, of feverish minds, or outbursts of passion.—Fear, terror, astonishment will cause a person to stop abruptly at every one, two, or three steps; or stagger a few steps forward and then backward.—Indecision, uncertainty, hesitation will be shown in walking to and fro, backward and forward—the direction of our steps, following the changing impulse of the mind.—Reflection is shown in frequent pauses.

## CHARACTERISTIC WALKS.

AFFECTED PRIDE.—Fig. 7 is the illustration of this sentiment.— The toes are conspicuously turned out; the leg is well straightened; the steps are slow and measured.—Leslie's picture of Malvolio gives the idea of this thoroughly.

VANITY.—The walk somewhat resembles that of Fig. 7, with this difference that the toes are more gracefully turned out.—The strides are rather shorter : a little more modesty is apparent in the general action, although the walk is at the same time strikingly typical of a man in love with his personal appearance (Fig. 8).

PRIDE OF PHYSICAL POWER.——Fig. 9 represents a man wh[o] [i]mpressing his arguments, relies more on the strength of hi[s] [a]nd muscular power than on his mental capacity. His feet [f]irm and flat on the ground. The man stands with his leg[s]

FIG. 8.                    FIG. 9.

apart—his walk is heavy and slow, and in that resembles normal state of his mind.

Walking on tiptoe is emblematic of mystery, discretion, curio[us] surprise (Fig. 10).—The toes turned in belong to persons who for some reason are absent-minded, or whose thoughts are preoccupied, —to men accustomed to reflection and study, therefore regardless of personal appearance.

Persons imbued with a sense of their own importance, such as country officials, or mayors, or any such small dignitaries, show their sense of authority by such deportment as shown in Figs. 11 and 12.

WALK OF A DRUNKARD. —The walk of a drunkard is, like his thoughts, disorderly—he steps forward, backward, right or left, trying in vain to keep his balance. His knees are always on the point of giving way. If he stands still, his toes and heels will indicate the movements of a ship pitching up and down. As there are many degrees of drunkenness, there are also many modifications to be observed in imitating a drunkard's walk. When the Count Almaviva, in the *Barber of Seville*, enters the house of Don Bartolo and demands a night's lodging, he assumes the demeanour of a drunken soldier—this walk will be uncertain and tottering, and yet it will be that of a gentleman.

FIG. 10.

Tragic actors are apt to walk so heavily that the whole of the body seems to receive a sort of concussion at each step. This

mars the harmony of their action and destroys the illusion of th
public, who see a stiff actor instead of one whose deportment i

FIG. 11.                      FIG. 12.

graceful and easy.   Others drag their toes on the ground, thu
assuming a pompous and ridiculous appearance (Fig. 13).

The walk of a drunkard offers such variety, and is so often misunderstood, that it would be too long a task to point out all the faults that should be avoided. We must therefore refer the reader to Chapter XIII., in which general observations are given.

Fig. 13.

# CHAPTER VI.

## THE HAND AND ARM.

MONTAIGNE has said :— "Quoy des mains? nous requérons, nous promettons, appelons, congédions, menaçons, prions, supplions, nions, refusons, interrogeons, admirons, nombrons, confessons, repentons, craignons, vergoignons, doutons, instruisons, incitons, encourageons, jurons, témoignons, accusons, condamnons, absolvons, injurions, méprisons, déffions, flattons, applaudissons, bénissons, humilions, moquons, réconcilions, recommandons, exaltons, festoyons, réjouissons, complaignons, attristons, déconfortons, désespérons, estimons, escrions, taisons ; et quoy non? d'une variation et multiplication à l'envy de la langue."

To sum up Montaigne's idea :—The formation of the hand is indeed the true reflector of our natural disposition. By its actions we betray our sentiments, our passions and aspirations.

If we study the figures in the following cuts we find the following expressions :—

Nos. 1 and 2.—Command, mingled with kindness. No. 3.—Consolation, gentle touching exhortations. No. 4.—Command, authority. No. 5.—Grace. No. 6.—Physical enjoyment. No. 7.—Gentle disposition. No. 8.—Elevated mind, taste, dexterity. No. 9.—Refinement. No. 10.—Persuasive eloquence, kindly pleading. No. 11.—Imploring. No. 12.—Energy, capable of great undertakings. No. 13.—Dignity, wisdom, experience.

Such expressions of hands as we see in these designs would not belong to coarse or low natures, nor yet to people employed in manual work. The exquisite harmony existing between all the fingers, as well as their graceful attitudes, denote gentle or noble sentiments. The thumb gives force and vigour to the hand : with it we tighten our grasp. A thin nervous thumb, capable of curving back, is emblematic of great refinement, and also of determination. The first finger or index is, after the thumb, the most useful part of the hand. Its freedom of articulation causes us to use it in almost every action of life. We point, command, work with it. What can be more graceful than the expression of the thumb and first finger in Fig. 11. The other three fingers, although they complete the harmonious formation of the hand, are only contributors, whilst the index and thumb are the most direct and useful agents of our actions.

No. 1.
Command mingled with kindness.

No. 2.
Command mingled with kindness.

No. 3.
Consolation, gentle touching
exhortation.

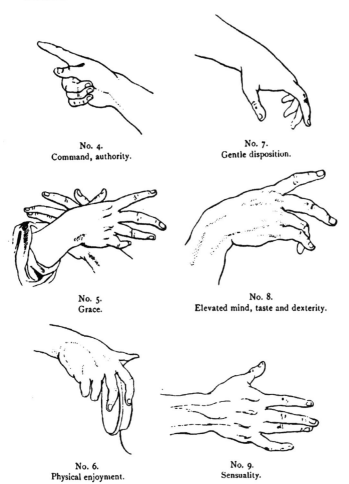

No. 4.
Command, authority.

No. 7.
Gentle disposition.

No. 5.
Grace.

No. 8.
Elevated mind, taste and dexterity.

No. 6.
Physical enjoyment.

No. 9.
Sensuality.

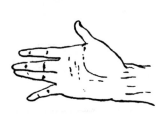

No. 10.
Persuasive eloquence, kindly
pleading.

No. 12.
Energy, capable of grea
undertakings.

No. 11.
Imploring.

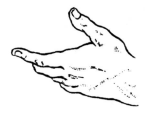

No. 13.
Dignity, wisdom, experience.

# CHAPTER VII.

## ACTIONS OF THE ARMS AND HANDS.

FIG. 14.

IT is obvious that our actions receive their impulse from our minds. If our thoughts take a certain direction, the body will naturally follow it. In addressing a person on our right hand, or if we wish to point or make a sign to the right, it would seem but natural that we should make use of the right hand : yet it is a very common fault amongst actors to ignore this impulse of nature, and do exactly the reverse, using the left hand whilst the body is turned to the right, and the right hand whilst the body turns to the left: thus assuming the very awkward position of Fig. 14.

We strongly advise students not to fall into this error.

The action of the arms follows the impulse of our

thoughts.    A calm thought will prompt a quiet action.    The arm will move slowly, without abruptness ; scarcely raised as in Fig. 15.

FIG. 15.

Such an action would correspond to such words like  these :—

" My friends, I come before you with this plea."

Should the thought assume more importance, the arms will be raised as in Fig. 16:—

FIG. 16.

"See, now, how good a thing is offered here."

D

Should the sentiment be strong, the thought will prompt the arm to rise rapidly, and assume at once an energetic expression ; (Figs. 17 and 18).

FIG. 17.

Fig. 17 would suggest the idea of religion enunciated with veneration, as in these lines :—

> "I have a brother is condemned to die ;
> I do beseech you, let it be his fault,
> And not my brother."

Fig. 18 appeals to Heaven to chastise the wicked. The feeling being much stronger, the hand is raised to its highest position, as in these lines :—

> " Heaven is above all yet : there sits a judge
> Whom no king can corrupt."

FIG. 18.

It is between the two extreme actions of Figs. 15 and 18 that the student must learn to express the numberless gradations of the different sentiments.

FIG. 19.

## PRELIMINARY STUDIES.

### FIRST PRACTICE.

The first study for the pupil will be to learn how to regulate the action of his arms and hands. Let us suppose the body in the second position. (Fig. 4), the arms hanging down perfectly loose and powerless. Imagine a string tied to the wrist and passed through a pulley secured to the ceiling.

In pulling that string gently, the hand will droop down and the arm will be gracefully rounded at the elbow as it is slowly raised. The pulling will cease as soon as the wrist is brought on a level with the chin; the hand will then raise itself slowly, and gently turn the palm upwards; when in that position, the hand, still sustained by the string, will fall naturally, as in Fig. 20,

FIG. 20.

FIG. 21.

the thumb extended without stiffness, and the fingers gracefully
rounded. As soon as this position
is obtained, the string will be lowered
very slowly, and as the arm resumes
its position, the palm of the hand
will gradually turn downward and
fall back to its former position, the
string being suddenly let loose, (Fig.
21).

This method of practising will teach the pupil how to raise and lower the arms and hands naturally and gracefully, and also to avoid the awkward actions of Figs. 22, 23, 24, 25.

FIG. 22.

FIG. 23.

FIG. 24.

SECOND PRACTICE.

The left arm and hand will then be submitted to the same
careful exercise.

FIG. 25.

# CHAPTER VIII.

EXPRESSION of favourable sentiments is given by the action of the arms and hands, the palm of the hands having a tendency upwards.

## THE PALM OF THE HAND.

We express our sentiments by the direction we give to the palm of the hand. If the sentiment we wish to indicate is favourable, the hand will take an upward direction, and the reverse where the sentiment is unfavourable. The hand repels with the palm, or protects with it the senses affected ; these gestures having a downward direction. On the contrary, in prayer, or the expression of friendship, love, &c., the hand displays the palm and assumes an upward direction.

All favourable sentiments are inspired by Heaven ; hence this tendency to direct our actions upwards, and also to turn towards the earth when prompted by our angry passions.

In order to attain perfect ease and freedom of action, we would recommend the pupil to express by appropriate actions of the hands as many different sentiments as possible, and in the following manner :—

## FIRST STUDY.

Suppose the pupil standing in the third position, between two
chairs placed in a line and intended to represent two persons; his

FIG. 26.

body will be three-parts turned towards the public, and he will
stand about one foot behind the line of the chairs, which are
 ·  ·ed at a distance of six feet from each other.   He will address

the person on his *right*, and his first movement will correspond to an impassioned expression, such as :

> " What you have spoke, it may be so, perchance."
>
> *Macbeth*.

The arm scarcely moved from the body; the palm of the hand slightly turned upward, the fingers bent without effort.

Fig. 26 is the quietest action that could possibly follow the entire repose of the body. Such a movement would correspond to gentle, calm sentiments, such as indifference, submission, esteem, veneration. The soul being in a state of repose prompts a corresponding action.

## SECOND STUDY.

Suppose that the sentiment to be expressed should assume a higher degree of intensity, the actions will become more decided : the hand will naturally be raised higher, whilst the arm will become slightly more distant from the body.

## GRADATION IN THE ACTIONS.

We may state that so long as in their movement the hands do not rise above the waist, they express sentiments of a quieter nature, such as we have stated in the above first study—but so soon as the hands are raised above the waist, and therefore reach the chest, which is the source whence spring all our sentiments, the centre of our activity, their expression assumes much greater force, much more intensity. The expression of the hands in Fig. 7 would correspond to the following sentiment :—

> " What you have said
> I will consider ; what you have to say,
> I will with patience hear."

The hand is raised higher, and the arm more distant from the body than in Fig. 26.

## THIRD STUDY.

The hand raised above the waist, the arms distant from the body, the fingers close together, and the palm of the hand well exposed to the view, as in Fig. 27,

FIG. 27.

all tend to express a strong sentiment, such as demand, request, equity, decision, assertion, &c.

"I shower a welcome on you ; welcome all !"

## FOURTH STUDY.

Where the sentiment is that of honour, of dignity, of pride, the hand will naturally cover the chest, Fig. 28.

FIG. 28.

This action might be appropriate to the following phrase :—
" And this, as from my very heart, I speak."

Although the palm of the hand is hidden in this action, yet we have introduced it in this chapter in order to show the gradual raising of the hands.

## FIFTH STUDY.

Sentiments of gratitude, kind wishes, love, admiration, will be expressed by a graceful combination of action. The hand will press

FIG. 29.

on the heart, and extend towards the object of our admiration; or else will be raised in a line with the chin, and, approaching the mouth convey by a gentle opening of the fingers and a graceful movement of the arms, the expression of our kind sentiments. The expression of the Figs. 29 and 30, would be admirably suited to this phrase :—

" Dear love, adieu !"

If our sentiments assume a sense of desire, the hand is naturally directed towards the coveted object, the arms stretch out, and the fingers curl up as in the act of receiving or grasping.

FIG. 30.

## SIXTH STUDY.

If one of our senses is excited, the hand following the impulse of our sentiment will be directed towards it, as in Fig. 31,

FIG. 31.

in the attitude of listening.   The palm of the hand is placed near the ear, as if to concentrate the sound.

" Hark ! Peace !
It was the owl that shrieked !"

## SEVENTH STUDY.

If our sentiments assume a nobler form such as the idea of
Heaven, our action will naturally be more elevated.

In speaking of Heaven as a collective idea of God, the action
will be somewhat similar to that of Fig. 32.

FIG. 32.

" And He that doth the ravens feed,
Yea, providently caters for the sparrow,
Be comfort to mine age ! "

If we appeal to Heaven itself, the action will not only be more energetic, but the first finger will point to the region where our imagination pictures the Deity to be (Fig. 18).

## EIGHTH STUDY.

The above studies will be repeated with the left hand.

## NINTH STUDY.

The pupil having acquired perfect ease, first with the right, and afterwards with the left hand, will repeat the same studies addressing the person on the right and on the left alternately,—advancing one, two, or more steps every time towards each chair. The walk will vary according to the sentiment to be expressed: that is, it will be slow and dignified, or short and abrupt.

# CHAPTER IX.

EXPRESSION of unfavourable sentiments—tendency of the palm of the hands downwards.

### FIRST STUDY.

Suppose the student standing in the second position, with his arms folded on his chest (Fig. 33), or hanging down, or crossed on his back.

FIG. 33.

When a sense of doubt or surprise rushes on us we instinctively stretch our hand out, the palm being turned downwards, the arm extending itself from the body, the fingers becoming slightly crooked, as in Fig. 34.

FIG. 34.

An unpleasant sight or a sudden disagreeable word, such as :—
"Though thou speakest truth,
Methinks thou speakest not well!"
would cause this action.

## SECOND STUDY.

If a sense of disgust, fear, contempt, anger, takes the place of doubt, the actions will be similar to those of Figs. 35, 36, 37, 38.

FIG. 35.

FIG. 36.

FIG. 37.                                    FIG. 38.

The two Figs. 37 and 38 combine the double actions of throw
ing the hand out, and then drawing it towards the body.   Th
idea is that of throwing away something that is distasteful.   Th
meaning of the double action is this : When putting our hand ou
quickly we throw as it were our contempt at others, and in with

drawing it towards us, we avoid a contact that might sully it.  If
we reverse the action of Fig. 38 and move the hand from the
body towards the person we address with abruptness, we obtain

FIG. 39.

equally an action suggestive of command mixed with contempt,
such as might be used by a superior towards a vassal—Fig. 39.

## THIRD STUDY.

Anger, as it becomes more violent and turns into a passion, will assume a different expression, and from attitude Fig. 38 will pass to that of Figs. 40 and 41.

FIG. 40.

The fist is closed tightly, the arm stretched out—it seems that the muscles of the body are rigid with the strength of our mental emotions. This action is emblematic of power, courage, defiance, or threat.

FIG. 41.

"Urge me no more—I shall forget myself!
 Have mind upon your health ;—tempt me no further !"

## FOURTH STUDY.

If fear assumes the form of terror or despair, the action will change from Fig. 36 into Figs. 42, 43, 44, and 45.

FIG. 42.

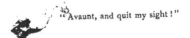

"Avaunt, and quit my sight!"

FIG. 43.

" Hence, horrible shadow !   unreal mockery, hence ! "

FIG. 44.

" Ah, whither shall I go? and which way fly?"

FIG. 45.

"My good Lord, that comfort comes too late,
For I am past all comfort here but prayers!"

## FIFTH STUDY.

FIG. 46.

"This fellow,
Let me ne'er see again."

The expression of Fig. 46 is that of authority, command, accusation.

F

Fig. 47.

"Take heed, my boy ;
I warn you, take good heed."

Fig. 47 is that of warning, reproach.　This action of the first finger,
is one of the most expressive motions we have, and is indicative of
an infinite variety of meanings.　A gentle movement of the hand,
while the arm is kept close to the body, means reproach—two or
three abrupt movements of the hand, and the arm more distant

from the body, mean scolding. One abrupt movement of the hand, the arm stretched, and the first finger pointed towards a person, means accusation; the same movement, with the forefinger pointing slightly to the ground, is also emblematic of command, authority. The simple shaking of the first finger means "beware." In comedy, the action of the first finger is often used in a figurative sense.

FIG. 48.

Fig. 48 means "doubt;" also the first finger bent, close beside the mouth, indicates perplexity or incredulity.

# CHAPTER X.

___

## PRELIMINARY PRACTICES FOR BOTH ARMS AND HANDS.

SYMMETRICAL movements in acting are admissible only in pantomimic action or low comedy, and are therefore incompatible with elevated sentiments. In high comedy or tragedy such movements would be out of place.

To express sentiments or passions, certain gradations must be observed in order to give them the desired intensity. In music we have the *piano, crescendo,* and *forte,* rendered by the combination of the different instruments ; in acting, we have the combination of the actions of the body, the expression of the face, and the *voice.* In this chapter we will consider the expression of the arms and hands. If we raise one hand, we give force to our words. By raising both, we give them additional expression. In order to obtain this *crescendo,* it is necessary to time these two actions, and graduate them, as will be explained in the following practices. The lowering of the arms corresponds to the *diminuendo* in music. We see in Figs. 22, 23, 24, 25, the absurdity of symmetrical movements, in which the hands are raised or extended at entirely equal angles from the body, the movements being likewise simultaneous, and keeping time with each other.

## FIRST PRACTICE.

Let the pupil stand in the second position —facing the audience. His first action will be to raise the right hand as high as the chest, which must be done according to the rules already stated in the first practice, Chapter VII. ; so soon as it will have ceased to rise, the left hand will follow the same movement, and cease ascending as soon as it has become level with the waist. By keeping one hand higher than the other, the pupil avoids symmetry in the position of the hands and arms, and by raising one after the other he obtains the desired gradation in the actions, or *crescendo*. The *diminuendo* of this action is the lowering of the arms, which movement takes place as soon as the sentiment diminishes from its intensity. In doing so, the pupil will lower, first the left hand and then the right, observing the same rules as above. The fact that the right hand is raised first and lowered last, and also that it is kept higher than the left, shows that it assumes the principal expression in the action, and therefore interprets the leading sentiment in a phrase. The importance of this observation will be fully exhibited in Chapter XXII., " Analysis of Mark Antony's Oration."

## SECOND PRACTICE.

The same practice will be repeated, giving the left hand the principal action.

---

*N.B.*—In Chapters XXII., XXIII., and XXIV., we shall give an analysis of the sentiments and passions with their different actions. As it will comprise the combined action of both hands and arms, we will limit the studies in this chapter to these two practices.

# CHAPTER XI.

―

## PHYSIOGNOMY.

LEBRUN said in one of his lectures that " Expression is, according to my opinion, a simple and natural reflection of the objects we have to represent." It is necessary it should exist between all the parts of a picture, which would be very imperfect without this condition. It also shows the movements of the soul and the effects of passion.

Lavater—from whom much of this chapter is derived, both as to remarks and illustrations—asserts that the head is the most noble and essential part of our bodily frame. It is the centre of our intellectual faculties. A head well-proportioned to the body, one that is neither too large nor yet too small, denotes a mind better balanced than could be expected from a head out of proportion. The forehead is the door of the soul ; the temple, the door of prudence.

The physiognomy, like the actions, has its typical features in every nation. The passions or sentiments are expressed very differently by people belonging respectively to northern and southern countries.

To understand the philosophy of human expression involves a study with which artists cannot dispense. A thorough acquaintance with the private character of the personage to be represented, and of the habits of the different countries and nationalities, are indispensable in order to obtain a perfect expression of physio-gnomy. The different stages of our life from youth to old age, as well as the nature of our occupations, all tend to leave a trace on our features; health, youth, beauty, joy, grief, misery, vanity, pride, suffering, decrepitude, all have their expression, all leave their marks. A quiet, serene life and a happy mind, develop a har-monious expression of feature, which, even in old age, indicates

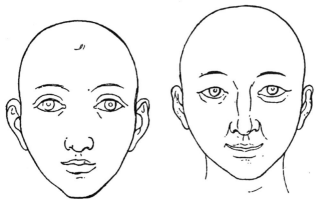

FIG. 1.—TRANQUILITY—CALM.          FIG. 2.—JOY.

cheerfulness and contentment. The reverse may be said where life has been spent amidst a storm of passions, or evil actions. The impassioned face of youth gradually loses its harmony: the lines in the face become harshly marked. The features betray anxiety, deceit, vice,—in one word, all the evil propensities of the soul.

Buffon declared that when the soul is quiet all the features of the face are in a state of perfect repose. Their harmonious com-bination indicates one gentle union of the thoughts, and corre-sponds to the internal calm.

When assuming an expression of a gentle sentiment, the lines of the face are raised slightly.

As the feeling increases in intensity, the features assume a brighter expression by an ascending movement.

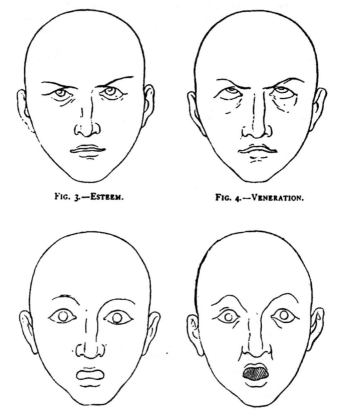

FIG. 3.—ESTEEM.

FIG. 4.—VENERATION.

FIG. 5.—ADMIRATION.

FIG. 6.—ASTONISHMENT.

So soon as the feeling becomes violent, the face loses its
harmonious lines, and the features assume different directions.
For instance, hearty laughter will cause the eyes to shut partly, if
not altogether, whilst the eyebrows will be raised.   The lines of
the face follow the direction of the mouth which opens at the
sides, assuming at the same time a cheerful expression by opening,
and thus exposing the teeth.

FIG. 7.—EAGERNESS.                          FIG. 8.—HOPE.

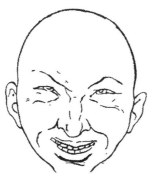

When our feelings become those of sorrow or suffering, the features are drawn downwards, always in proportion to the intensity of our sensations.

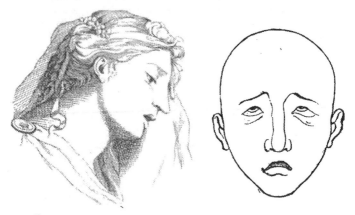

FIG. 10.          FIRST MOVEMENT OF GRIEF.          FIG. 11.

So soon as the sensation becomes violent, the features are drawn apart, upwards and downwards, assuming opposite directions, and becoming distorted; in fact they reflect, like a true mirror, the state of the soul.

The following figures all tend to show violent passions or suffering :—

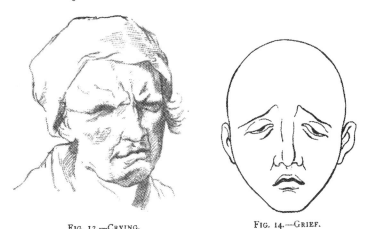

FIG. 13.—CRYING.                    FIG. 14.—GRIEF.

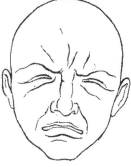

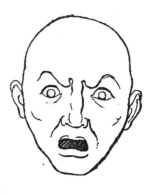

FIG. 16.—EXTREME DESPAIR.

FIG. 17.
SURPRISE MIXED WITH FRIGHT.

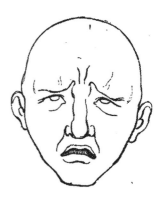

FIG. 18.—ANGER MIXED WITH FEAR.

FIG. 19.
ACUTE BODILY AND MENTAL PAIN.

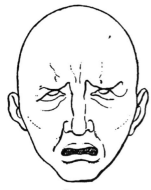

FIG. 20.
COMPOUND MOVEMENT OF PAIN.

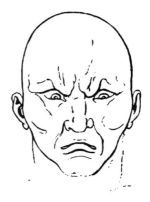

FIG. 21.
VIOLENT MOVEMENT.

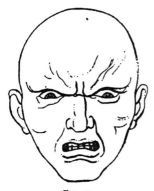

FIG. 22.
OTHER KIND OF VIOLENT MOVEMENT.

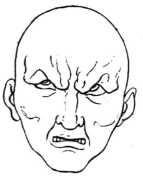

FIG. 23.—VIOLENT MOVEMENT.
CONTRACTION OF THE HEART.

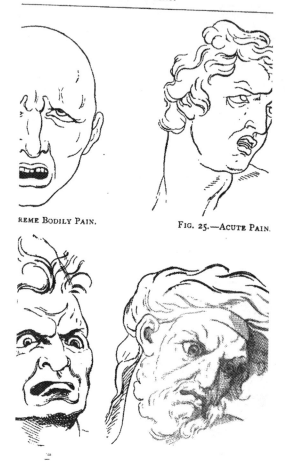

REME BODILY PAIN.

FIG. 25.—ACUTE PAIN.

ANGER.

FIG. 27.—OTHER KIND OF ANGE

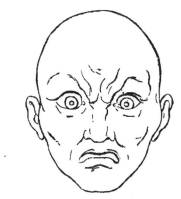

Fig. 28.—Horror.

Fig. 29.—Fright.

FIG. 30.—ANOTHER KIND OF FRIGHT.

FIG. 31.—FEAR.                    FIG. 32.—JEALOUSY.

FIG. 33.—HATRED.          FIG. 34.—FRIGHT MIXED WITH ANGER.

When the face assumes the expression of a violent passion, the mouth is often opened. This movement may easily be explained by the fact that the action of the heart is strongly affected, and the breathing being interrupted by emotion, is therefore facilitated by this action. We see by the above observations that when sentiments assume a mild form the features of the face retain a symmetrical expression, in an upward or downward direction. On the contrary, if the emotions of the mind are violent, the features become disordered and take all sorts of directions, viz., upwards, downwards, and lateral. The former class of feelings are therefore expressed by *similar*, the latter by *contrary* motions.

The student will do well to analyse these different expressions, which represent the various sentiments or passions of the soul. Having done so, it would be advisable for him to imitate them before a looking-glass. An actor will never become a great artist unless he expresses by the actions of his physiognomy the passions which are supposed to agitate his soul. If he remains impassible when his features ought to reflect the joyful or tortured state of his inward feelings, he will fail to influence or attract an enlightened or intelligent public. We have stated that the features assume the same direction in quiet sentiments, and opposite directions as they grow in intensity. This latter action, however, is observable in states of mind which are composed of two simultaneous contrary sentiments. For instance, the lover who is wrapped up in the thoughts of the absent object of his affections is besieged by conflicting sentiments of pleasure and pain. The physiognomy is expressive of both in the following manner—the upper part of the face is affected by the feeling of grief, whilst the lower part reflects the sensation of love. The eyes are either shut, or languishing, or even shedding tears. The eyebrows are raised at the corners near the bridge of the nose, as though casting a shadow on it, whilst a smile gives the mouth a gentle expression of happiness. A touching melody or a sublime musical conception often causes a concentrated sentiment of rapture, which assumes the above outward expression. We may conclude from these observations, that in sentiments expressed by contrary actions, the upper part of the face assumes the expression of unfavourable whilst the lower part assumes that of favourable sentiments. Not only does the general appearance of the physiognomy show the general dispositions of human beings, but each one of the features denotes our peculiar propensities. A hooked nose, with a thick lip, generally belong to the miser; a small restless eye that never looks you in the face is often characteristic of hypocrisy. It is necessary that actors should become acquainted with all the peculiarities of the face and understand their meaning. We will, therefore, analyse them, and quote some of Lavater's observations on physiognomy.

## THE FOREHEAD.

The long part of the forehead, its form, height, curve and proportions, mark the disposition and the measure of our intellectual faculties, our way of thinking and feeling. The skin of the forehead, its position, colour, tension, or looseness, betrays the passions of the soul, the normal state of our mind. In one word, the solid part of the forehead indicates the measure of our intellectual faculties and the mobile part the use we make of them. The solid part always remains in the same state, while the exterior covering or skin gets wrinkled, in the course of time, or by the effect of thought, care, sorrow, &c.

The lines vary according to the form of the bony structure. On a flat forehead they are different from those belonging to an arched forehead. Therefore, if we consider them in an abstract manner, they enable us to judge of the form of the forehead; and, on the other hand, we may be able to determine according to its form, the lines that will be produced.

Wrinkles may be perpendicular, horizontal, arched, or interlaced and complicated.

The foreheads that are smooth produce simple and regular lines.

A narrow forehead is indicative of an unruly mind.

A forehead sinking in the lower part and prominent in the

upper part, shows stupidity, cowardice, incapacity for great under-takings.

A square forehead is indicative of wisdom and firmness (Fig. 35).

FIG. 35.
GREAT MEMORY—FIRMNESS—LEARNING.

An elevated and round forehead denotes an open, virtuous man, susceptible of gratitude and of kind sentiments.

A badly-shaped forehead without wrinkles betrays a rough, fighting disposition, wanting in intelligence.—See Figs. 36 to 41 for different shaped foreheads.

FIG. 36.—SAGACITY.

FIG. 37.—KINDNESS.

FIG. 38.—PERSPICACITY.

FIG. 39.—AVARICE.

FIG. 40.—SHREWDNESS MIXED WITH HYPOCRISY.

FIG. 41.—DARK SOUL.
SLIGHT CONTRACTION OF THE LIPS.

## THE EYES.

Buffon says—"It is chiefly in the eyes that are pictured the images of our secret agitations, and there they can be recognised. The eye belongs to the soul more than any organ—it seems to touch it and participate in all its movements—it expresses its most vivid passions, and its most disorderly emotions, as well as

FIG. 42.
SIR C. WREN.

the gentlest and most delicate sentiments. It expresses them in all their force—in all their purity, the instant they are felt. It renders them with vivid flashes and impresses us with the very fire, actions, and images of the sentiments they reflect. The eye receives and flashes forth at the same time the light of

thoughts and the warmth of sentiment.  It is the sense of the
spirit, and the tongue of the sentient intelligence."

In the figures shown in Figs. 1 to 34, we see the expression
of the eyes varying from perfect repose to the utmost excess of
passion.

In the portrait of Sir C. Wren (Fig. 42), we see a noble
expression—the right eye especially—betrays worlds of intelligence.  Such an expression can belong only to a man gifted
with extraordinary talent.

Fig. 43.

Fig. 43 denotes great expression in the eyes.

## THE EYEBROWS.

The eyebrows are positive indicators of a man's character.

Eyebrows softly arched are among the charms of a modest and simple young girl, (Fig. 44).

FIG. 44.

When they form a straight and horizontal line, the eyebrows denote a firm and vigorous mind, (Fig. 45).

FIG. 45.—CH. CH. REISEN.

When partly horizontal and partly arched (curved), they denote firmness united with ingenuous kindness (Fig 46).

FIG. 46.—A. HONDIUS.

Rough and ragged eyebrows generally betray an uncontrolled quickness of temper; if, however, the hair is fine, it is the sign of a moderately fiery disposition (Fig. 47).

FIG. 47.—SENECA.

Thick and compact eyebrows, with the hairs bent in a parallel direction, as though they were brushed down in a straight line, are generally the sign of a solid and mature judgment, of wisdom, of healthy and practical common-sense.— (Fig. 48.)

FIG. 48.

When they are thin, it is a sign of weakness or of phlegmatic indifference.

When angular and irregular, they denote a prolific mind (Fig. 49).

FIG. 49.—QUESNOY.

Drooping eyebrows give to the head an appearance of sadness and melancholy.   When joined together over the nose they give the face a surly look, betraying to a certain degree an unsettled mind; although this formation is considered by some people as a sign of beauty.   Such eyebrows might also belong to amiable dispositions.

The nearer they are to the eyes, the more firmness of mind do they indicate.   The energy diminishes as they gradually ascend.

A great distance between the eyebrows is considered a sign of an easy temperament, a calm and tranquil soul.

White eyebrows show a feeble temperament, dark brown are emblematic of strength.

The movements of the eyebrows vary infinitely, and serve chiefly to mark all the violent passions of the soul.

A man who frowns betrays an unsettled state of mind.

Lebrun says—"There are two sorts of movements in the eyebrows,—the one, when they are raised in the middle, expresses favourable sentiments; in this case the mouth is drawn up at the sides. The other, when they are lowered in the middle, denotes grief or bodily pain; in this case the corners of the mouth are drawn down."

In laughter, all the features move in the same direction—the eyebrows being lowered towards the middle of the forehead cause the nose, the mouth, the cheeks, to follow the same movement.

## THE NOSE.

A handsome nose is rarely seen on a face devoid of harmonious forms, or on a deformed face. A person may be plain or ugly and possess fine eyes; but a regular nose necessarily involves a harmonious analogy and proportion of the other features. We see thousands of handsome eyes to one handsome nose; which feature, when it is really well formed, generally denotes an excellent disposition and a distinguished mind.

A handsomely-formed nose must have the following qualities— Its length must be equal to that of the forehead, and it must be slightly curved at the bridge. Seen in the full face, its ridge must be moderately broad, and parallel on both sides; its breadth must be slightly more marked towards the middle.

The end of the nose must be neither hard nor fleshy: the lower outline must be well defined correctly and with precision, that is, neither too sharp nor yet too broad. The sides of the nose must present a distinct form, and the nostrils assume an agreeable curve as they shorten themselves in the upper part. Seen in profile, the base of the nose must not exceed a third of its length.

Yet many people of the greatest merit possess a badly-shaped

H

nose. In this case it is necessary to distinguish the kind of merit which characterises them. For instance, a nose arched in its upper part near the forehead, denotes an imperative and arbitrary disposition, as seen in the effigies of the Romans and the Normans. A nose with a straight well-defined ridge shows an energetic mind, a character able to act, and to suffer silently. A nose with a broad ridge denotes superiority: when very narrow near the forehead, it shows extraordinary but fitful energy. A small nostril is the sign of timidity. When the nostrils are well opened and sensitive to the action of the breath, they denote refined sentiments. See the following figures.

PERFECTION OF NOSE.

RESOLUTION.

BRUTALITY.

FIRMNESS.

ORDER.

TIMIDITY.                    ENERGY.

## THE CHEEKS.

Fleshy cheeks indicate in general a mild temperament and a sensual appetite. When thin and shrunk, they are a sign of a rigid temperament, one little addicted to the enjoyment of life. Grief makes the cheeks hollow; vulgarity and stupidity stamp them with coarse lines. Slight and undulating lines are a sign of wisdom and refinement.

A cheek gracefully formed denotes a sensitive and generous heart, incapable of a mean action.

Beware of a man whose smile is not genuine. A graceful smile is the true barometer of a kind heart and a noble mind.

## THE CHIN.

A projecting chin is the sign of a positive mind, whilst a retreating chin indicates weakness and deficiency. Thus, the energy or weakness of a person is often exclusively indicated by the chin.

Sharp indentations in the middle of the chin seem to indicate a judicious man, possessed of calm understanding, and resolute; a sharp chin shows acuteness and craft.

A double chin, soft and fleshy, is generally a sign of sensuality or indolence.

Angular chins belong, as a rule, to discreet, firm, and well-disposed persons.

Flat chins indicate a cold or dry temperament.

Small chins indicate timidity; and the round chins with a dimple are typical of kindness.

## THE MOUTH AND LIPS.

The mouth is the interpreter and representative of the mind, of the heart : whether in repose or in its infinitely varied action, it comprises a *world* of characteristic features. It is eloquent in its very silence.

Well-marked or chiselled and well-proportioned lips, which present on either side the middle line equally well arched, are incompatible with a low, false, unkind, or mean mind.

A mouth tightly closed, which at the junction of the lips forms a straight line, indicates a cold, collected mind, application, a tendency to order, punctuality, method.

If the mouth is drawn up at the two extremities, it shows a certain amount of affectation, pretension, vanity, and malice, which is the ordinary result of frivolity.

Fleshy lips are the emblems of sensuality, laziness; round and thick lips denote timidity and avarice.

Lips that close gracefully without tightness, and form regular lines, indicate a judicious, firm, thoughtful mind.

A slightly overhanging upper lip is often a distinctive sign of kindness. A projecting under lip belongs to a calm, sincere, easy mind rather than a very tender heart.

A lower lip which becomes hollow in the middle, belongs to a cheerful and fanciful person. This expression is perceptible after a joke or witty remark.

A mouth well closed without affectation, and not sharp or pointed, shows courage.

An opened mouth betrays sorrow, and sometimes vacancy of mind.

A closed mouth shows patient suffering.

IDIOTCY.

KINDNESS.

STUPIDITY.

VULGARITY.

QUICK TEMPER.

IRASCIBILITY.

GENIUS MIXED WITH
KINDNESS.

GOOD SENSE.

MODERATELY SENSIBLE.

## THE TEETH.

Nothing is more characteristic, more striking than the teeth, if we consider their shape, and the way in which they are set. Small short teeth, in adults, show great strength, or great penetration. In neither case are they very fine or white. Long teeth betray weakness or timidity. White teeth regularly set and not always discovered, and which when the mouth is opened show themselves without projecting, indicate in adults a gentle and polished mind, a kind and brave heart.

When any of the front teeth are missing, it ages the face and alters the expression of the mouth unfavourably. In making up for some characters, some of the front teeth are occasionally blackened, to give the appearance of age.

## THE EARS.

When the ears are long or project outward from the head it is advisable to hide them under the hair. A small and well-shaped ear adds as much grace to the physiognomy, as an abnormally large, and badly-shaped one, destroys its harmony and proportion.

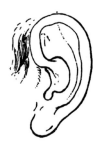

WIT AND REFINEMENT.

## THE HAIR.

The hair shows by many different signs the temperament of human nature, its sensitiveness, energy, and its various mental faculties. It corresponds to our physical constitution as plants and fruits correspond to the soil that produces them. Long hair denotes an effeminate temperament. No doubt it was in this sense that St Paul said that it was discreditable for a man to cultivate his hair—and in the same way the Puritans declaimed against the flowing locks of the Cavaliers. Straight and long hair does not show a manly disposition. Irregular short and straight hair is considered as a type of vulgarity—also the hair that falls in small sharp unpleasant-looking curls, especially when the texture is coarse and of a dark brown. This is typical of the lower class.

Hair of a golden hue or light brown, almost fair, slightly glossy, and graceful in its undulations, is considered very handsome.

Black hair, growing close to the head, thick and rather coarse, and naturally curly, shows little mental power, but, at the same time, application and order. It has been said that straight-haired men have ruled the world.

Black thin hair on a head partly bald, with an elevated and well-arched forehead, is indicative of great judgment, although with a want of inventive power, or of ready wit. On the contrary, the same kind of hair when it is flat and smooth, shows a decided weakness in the intellectual faculties. In warm countries the hair is of deepest black—less so or even brown in temperate climates. In cold countries the tints vary between yellow and brown. In old age these different colours turn to grey and white.

Fair hair generally denotes a gentle disposition, also a confident, phlegmatic temperament. Red hair denotes a man as either very kind or very cruel. Beware of a person who shows a striking contrast between the colour of the eyebrow and that of the hair. The diversity existing between the coats of hair in animals shows how expressive the diversity of hair must be in human beings. If we compare the wool of the lamb with the fur of the wolf; the coat of the hare with that of the hyena ; the feathers of the different birds, we cannot deny the fact that these differences are characteristic and enable us to judge of the inclinations and habits of each animal. It is most interesting, in reading the history of the habits of different nations, to see the importance that was attached to the beauty, length, cut, and disposition of the hair. Oriental nations cut or shave off the hair, their heads being covered with large turbans. With the inhabitants of cold regions, the hair is the principal covering for the head. Amongst the ancient Gauls, and also among the Germanic nations, the length of the hair was the distinctive sign of freedom and nobility. Cæsar caused the heads of the Gauls to be shaved after conquering them. Pharamond, chief of the Gauls, was surnamed "Rex Crinitus." To shave the hair of a prince was to degrade him. Under Louis XIV., it was the fashion to wear enormous wigs, and the king was never seen, even by his most intimate associates, without his peruke. These wigs gave an air of dignity to those who wore them. His hairdresser, "Binette," stated that he would willingly have shaved all the subjects to ornament the head of the master. At the present day, lawyers and judges make use of wigs, as it gives them a graver appearance than a bald head. See Figs. 50, 51, 52, and 53 for different expressions of faces.

FIG. 50.—ENERGY MINGLED WITH SENSUALITY.

Fig. 51.

Fig. 52.

Idiots.

FIG. 53.—WIT AND TASTE.

# CHAPTER XII.

---

## ON PASSIONS AND FEELINGS.

### PRELIMINARY OBSERVATIONS.

ROSCIUS and Cicero challenged each other as to which of them would render the same thought with the greatest variety—the former in words, the latter in actions. This illustrates the fact that by a slight modification of actions and words, we can obtain an infinite number of combinations to express the same sentiment.

In the following chapters, we shall analyse the different passions and feelings, and classify them according to their characteristic features. We shall also indicate the attitudes and actions suitable for each of them. We can of course only give general rules; it will be for the student to combine and modify the expressions according to his nature, and also to the requirements of the part he is representing.

### ANALYSIS OF FEELINGS AND CONDITIONS OF MIND, EXPRESSED BY THE GENERAL ATTITUDE OF THE BODY.

I. DIGNITY.—The sentiment of dignity may be suggested either by consciousness of merit, power, rank, titles, education, refinement of mind, or any similar cause, which prompts us to look upon others, or consider matters, from a higher position or point of view.

The attitude and action appropriate to this sentiment would be these : the head and body must be erect, the walk rather slow, the steps long and regular, the toes slightly turned outward, the movement of the hands slow and grave. At times one of the hands will be placed high on the breast, under the coat or waistcoat, whilst the other hand will either rest on the back, or hang motionless by the side of the body.

The face assumes a kind, although serious, expression.

Dignity in its manifestation suggests great regularity of features. The higher our station in life is, the more dignity we observe in all our actions, Fig. 28, page 63.

II. PRIDE.—This sentiment is prompted by causes based more on natural gifts such as beauty, strength, &c., or circumstantial advantages such as rank or fortune, than on a consciousness of real merit. We might almost say that this feeling is the result of ignorance, or of an ill-balanced mind. The attitude of the proud man, and also his gestures, resemble the signs that indicate dignity, only with the addition of marks of affectation ; such as we see in Fig. 7, page 37. His features assume the expression of contempt or self-complacency ; his head is thrown back, he addresses others with scorn, staring at them from head to foot as though taking a survey of their inferiority. Thus, Glenalvon, in the tragedy of "*Douglas*," reproaching young Norval for pride, says,

" If you presume
To bend on soldiers those disdainful eyes,
As if you took the measure of their minds,
And said in secret, ' You're no match for me,'
What will become of you?"

He is so wrapped up in his own importance that he scarcely condescends to lend any attention to others, or favour them with an answer. The action of the arms and hands is studied and unnatural, the steps are long and measured, the toes extremely turned out. Fig. 7, page 37, represents a man proud of his personal appearance; Fig. 11, page 41, the pride of rank. The pride of physical power would correspond to the attitude of Fig. 12, page 41.

III. VANITY.—This sentiment resembles pride in a milder form, and is suggested by the same causes. It is an attribute of gentle or weak minds, who attach great importance to physical appearance, and are more addicted to futile occupations than to serious pursuits. The action expressing this sentiment may be graceful, although studied, and calculated to make a certain impression on others. Whistling, humming, smiling on the slightest provocation, turning the head to the right and left, swinging the body in walking, taking short and graceful steps, throwing the arms forward so as to show the white cuffs, curling the moustache, or passing the hand through the hair, are gestures well suited to this sentiment; Fig. 8, page 39, is a good illustration of the vain man.

IV. DEFIANCE.—The expression of this feeling varies greatly. It may assume the form of brutality or of dignity. A threat addressed to a man of education will be met with a dignified countenance, and a brave attitude and look will express that the recipient sets his antagonist at defiance, daring him to carry it out.

On the other hand, a man of a lower stamp will defy his enemy with a very different action; his face will express anger, his attitude will display his combative power. Fig. 9, page 39, shows a man ready to fight. The legs are wide apart, the feet are firmly set on the ground, the fists closed, the head sunk deep between the shoulders, all these are signs typical of this sentiment in such a man.

V. INDOLENCE.—This sentiment betrays a passive and languid state of mind, incapable of energetic purpose: too idle to make the slightest effort. The movements of an indolent man indicate his apathetic frame of mind. The hands are plunged in his pockets, or fall listlessly to his sides; the knees are loose and ready to give way; the feet drag on the ground. In one word, the whole of his frame seems about to succumb from mere want of purpose. The face assumes a stupefied or vapid, inane expression, all intelligence having disappeared from the countenance.

VI. INDIFFERENCE. — This sentiment springs from various causes. The mind becomes callous after a succession of adverse circumstances, or may be so naturally. In both cases it will reject all emotions, taking an easy and careless view of passing events. Indifference is often the result of selfishness. The indifferent man is not easily affected by others' misfortunes or happiness. Either his want of intelligence shuts up his senses to anything outside the range of his conception, or his hardened soul is incapable of further emotion; or, perhaps again, his selfishness and egotism will render him indifferent to all things unconnected with his own interests. The shrugging of the shoulders and apathy of expression in the face would express this state of mind.

VII. DREAMY THOUGHTFULNESS; ABSENCE OF MIND. — People who are in the habit of dreaming are, as it were, in contemplation of their own idle thoughts. The mind is absent, and seems to ignore whatever is going on. The eyes assume a vacant expression; they are fixed, although they may not be attracted by any particular object. Again, this sentiment may be caused by a sense of admiration; then the effects are very different. The expression of the face denotes much more vivacity; the eyes, although fixed, not only retain their intelligence but become far more vivid, if the cause of contemplation is highly gratifying to the mind. Veneration will also cause this sentiment. In this case the face assumes a languid and sad expression. The arms folded on the chest, or crossed on the back, a motionless attitude, either standing or sitting, would correspond with this sentiment.

VIII. REFLECTION OR THOUGHT.—This sentiment is the result of an active mind, and although springing from the same source, yet is rendered by actions and attitudes different in their expression. A person who has a pursuit in life, and follows the same idea, shows a regularity and steadiness of thought by attitudes and actions of the same nature. The walk and movements

are quiet and unassuming. The face is serious; the eyes penetrat-
ing and thoughtful; at the same time the features preserve their
harmony as the mind is not disturbed from its ordinary course.
On the contrary, if thoughts of an unusual kind assail the mind
and offer cause of disturbance, the outward action and the
physiognomy assume at once a very different expression.

If the flow of ideas is checked by some difficult question, the
movements become nervous. If sitting, the man passes his hand
across his forehead; he leans back in his chair, as if seeking
inspiration in the air; he folds his arms on his chest; he rests his
elbows on the table, and his head is buried in his hands; in fact,
there is a frequent change of attitude until a solution of the
problem has restored the balance of the mind. A restless movement of the fingers, such as putting the forefinger on the lips, or
fidgetting with the leaves of a book or with a pen, would also
belong to the expression of this sentiment.

If walking, the steps will be irregular, the movements abrupt,
following the impulse of a mind which pursues an interrupted
course of ideas. Walking slowly, then quickly, stopping suddenly,
striking the forehead, folding the arms on the chest, would be the
appropriate actions of the body; whilst the eyebrows will be
lowered over the eyes, causing at the same time a slight frown and
betraying great concentration of thought.

Portia, in *Julius Cæsar*, says to Brutus—

> " Yesternight at supper
> You suddenly arose and walked about,
> Musing and sighing with your arms across."

IX. PRUDENCE.—This sentiment is the result of wisdom and
reflection. A prudent man never acts on the impulse of the
moment, but weighs matters before coming to a determination.
He is careful of his words, so as not to give offence by indiscreet
observations. His gestures are moderate, his manner unassuming, although dignified. The expression of his face is authoritative and kind at the same time. One of the gestures appropriate
to this sentiment is the authoritative movement of the forefinger,
which, being put forward is the emblem of caution and warning.

No precipitation betrays itself, either in the walk or in the motions of the arms, nor yet in the mode of speaking.

X. INDECISION.—This sentiment is the consequence of caution or prudence, or the result of want of intellectual power.

A vigorous mind is rarely undecided. This feeling is expressed by gestures and looks very different from those that indicate prudence. Timidity or uncertainty in the movements, such as an irregular or interrupted walk, or the steps taking different directions, the hands moved in all sorts of ways, first scratching the head, then the face, or rubbed together; the head nodding first in acquiescence, then shaking in negation. All these features belong to minds incapable of making a determination or carrying out any plan with a clear understanding.

XI. TIMIDITY.—This sentiment, which is caused by what may be called a want of nerve, is one of the characteristic features of women in general and of effeminate minds; and yet it is frequently observed in men gifted with great intellectual power and capable of energetic undertakings. In the former it is noticeable in the attitude and manner in general.

The action of the arm and the hand is reserved—scarcely perceptible. The walk is very short and quick. A timid person is never free from a certain amount of fear and indicision—a word, a look, will cause a blush. The speech is delivered in a subdued tone, as though the very sound of the voice gave cause of alarm. The eyes are kept down, for fear of meeting the gaze of others. The face retains a quaint soft expression, incapable of reflecting decided or deep feeling.

When affecting great minds, timidity may be considered as a failing, caused as much by modesty as by want of nerve. The consciousness of our deficiencies in certain matters invariably causes timidity when we have to deal with these matters in the presence of others.

XII. AUDACITY. — This sentiment, being the reverse of timidity, will assume the very opposite outward expression. Insolence may be coupled with defiance, accompanied by their exuberance of actions, and violence in the attitude.

I

XIII. COURAGE.—This noble sentiment belongs to a man gifted with an energetic, fearless disposition. Courage is often accompanied by intellectual power, although it is not necessarily so. The very instinct of self-preservation gives courage to animals. Some men may be totally destitute of mental strength, and yet be brave and courageous, whilst a military man, who by his capacities as a tactician, and his dauntless bravery has gained rank and honours, will unite this sentiment to great mental qualifications. True courage not only despises brutality but is associated with generous sentiments; yet these sentiments are due more to a sense of honour than of tenderness, for the man capable of braving danger is not so easily accessible to tender feelings. The expression of the physiognomy has a tendency to severity if not harshness. The action of the body and the general attitude are decided and full of vigour. The eyes express energy and command.

# CHAPTER XIII.

PASSIONS AND FEELINGS—*continued.*

EAGERNESS, IN VARIOUS PHASES.

INTRODUCTORY.

A POSITION of the body inclined forward is the very first expression of this sentiment, which directs all our actions towards the object of our desires. If one of our senses is affected by eagerness more than the others, it becomes the centre of our actions. If it is the sight, the eyes assume a greater expression of vivacity, the head leans forward, the hand naturally shades the brow so as to check the action of the light; if the ear is eager, the hand places itself behind it so as to concentrate the sound, the body leaning forward in the direction which attracts the attention, Fig. 31, page 66. If in the act of taking or receiving, the hands show great readiness of action, the expression of the fingers in either of these acts becomes very striking; if the desire is great, the face becomes flushed, the eyebrows are slightly moved, the mouth opens gently, the whole physiognomy displays a sense of uncontrollable longing, Fig. 7, Chap. XI., page 89. If this sentiment becomes a passion, it assumes the different forms which we shall find analysed in this chapter.

I. CURIOSITY. — This sentiment is caused· by the extreme
eagerness·of our mind to become acquainted with everything that
passes.   Its motives may be idle or the reverse.   Some people
have a natural desire to become acquainted with everybody's
business without any special motives ; others are ready at all
times to turn their knowledge to account.   This sentiment, carried
to excess, becomes indiscretion.   There is no special action to
express it, except a certain activity of mind which betrays itself in
the face and in the movements of the body.   The former assumes
a look of eagerness and hope, such as we see represented in Figs.
7 and 8, Chap. XI., page 89.   The action would be the same as
that which expresses those two sentiments.   Or, if the cause of
this feeling appeals more to one sense than the other, the features
belonging to that sense become very pronounced in their expression, and the action is concentrated as already stated in the
earlier part of this chapter.

II. INDISCRETION.—This feeling is prompted by a sense of
curiosity and assumes the same expression.   An indiscreet person
will not only ask questions, but will even insist on knowing the
why and the wherefore of everything, though at the risk of causing
pain and annoyance.   A want of reflection or an ingredient of
selfishness often causes this sentiment ; listening at the door,
looking through the keyhole, are actions typical of indiscreet and
prying curiosity.

III. EXPECTATION.—This feeling assumes the expression of
hope, anxiety, uncertainty, grief, impatience, according to the
nature of the thing expected.   The expectation of news, good or
bad, of the arrival of a beloved or a dreaded person, will cause a
series of gestures belonging to either of these sentiments.   To
render it adequately, we must be thoroughly imbued with the
cause of this sentiment.   If it is connected with auspicious events,
the action will be that expressive of favourable sentiments.   If, on
the contrary, it is caused by unfavourable circumstances, the
expressions will assume such features as may be suggested by a
disordered state of the mind.   In either case, eagerness is the
promoter of our action.   In the players' scene, Hamlet suppresses

all outward show of gestures. although watching the king's countenance with the utmost eagerness, expecting every instant to see
him betray the terror of his guilty conscience. A slight nervous
action of the hands, and the terrible expression of his eyes, indicate the intensity of his feelings. The expression of the face
corresponds to that of hatred or fear. Fig. 31, page 66, corresponds to the attitude of a person who tries to hear the slightest
sound, such as the steps of a beloved one.

The head and body incline towards the direction where we
expect to hear the sound; one of the hands is raised close to the
ear, whilst the other stretches out as if to repel or check any
strange noise, or to impose silence on any one who should venture
to speak.

IV. GLUTTONY.—The man whose sense of appetite is strongly
developed makes a god of his stomach. His thoughts are concentrated on the one object—the joy of eating. He lives to eat!
His expression is, like his mind, essentially material. His
physiognomy lacks intelligence. His eyes are sunk, and gloat
over his food as he puffs out his fat cheeks. The sight of a well-
dressed dish will cause a smile of satisfaction. When sitting at a
dinner table, he rubs his hands in anticipation of the pleasure to
come. He scarcely takes notice of what is said to him. His
eyes watch the choicest morsels; his attention is concentrated on
his plate. A gourmand generally eats slowly, so as to relish every
mouthful. He fills his glass to the brim, and puts it to his lips
slowly, so as not to lose a drop. In drinking the generous wine
he shuts his eyes and after emptying the glass, he makes a slight
noise with his tongue as a sign of approbation. He invariably
puts the glass to his nose so as to enjoy the bouquet of the wine.
He passes his fork from the left to the right hand, after cutting his
meat, so as not to hurry over his food, and that he may enjoy it
all the longer. He generally takes pretty large pieces, so that his
palate may appreciate the full flavour of the viands. Rather than
lose any part of it, he delicately takes the bone between his
fingers, and cleans it of all its covering; after which he sucks his
fingers previous to his wiping them on the napkin. The hands of

the gourmand are generally white and fat, as they do but very little work. The steps of the gourmand are generally short, like those of fat people, and slow, as his energy betrays itself more by the activity of his jaws than by that of any other part of his body.

V. DRUNKENNESS.—If the sense of gluttony betrays a sensual disposition, the passion for drink denotes a degraded mind. This passion has its own exclusive expression, for it announces its presence by unmistakable signs. To some it gives corpulence and colour, others it poisons; with the former it becomes a weakness, in the latter it is an inveterate vice. The effect of drink on people is so varied that its expressions are indeed endless. They assume the forms of all the sentiments and passions conceivable. The contrast in a man when sober and when drunk is very striking. Some become amazingly tender and sentimental under the vinous influence, others quarrelsome or given to moralising, whereas they have proved to be the very reverse when in a sober state.

The inveterate drunkard retains a fair amount of control over his countenance, and will walk almost steadily, whereas an occasional drinker will lose all power over his limbs.

One of the finest scenes of drunkenness we ever witnessed was at the Théâtre Français, in Paris, in "*l'Aventurière,*" when Coquelin (who performs the part of Don Annibal, brother to the aventurière) is seated with Fabrice at a breakfast table. Whilst his guest pours the wine in his tumbler, he holds it with a firm grip until it is full to the brim : then he approaches it carefully to his lips, and for fear of spilling a single drop he advances his mouth towards the cup, projects his lips until they have reached it, and as he empties it he throws his head gradually back until the whole contents have gone down his throat, the mouth clinging to the goblet, and giving evident signs of activity all the time the beverage is being absorbed. After several bumpers he becomes communicative, betrays the secrets of his sister's former calling, wishes to embrace his companion for whom he declares the most profound feeling of affection, until he bursts into tears, overcome by his own emotions ; at last he falls back in his chair dead asleep.

The whole of this scene was perfectly natural; no coarseness, no vulgarity of any sort. Indeed it was a masterpiece of acting.

VI. AVARICE.—The intense eagerness for accumulating wealth is the predominating and ruling passion of the miser. Such is its intensity that to obtain his object he will resort to the most illegitimate means. The expression of this passion might be rendered by the following features. A small quick eye, sunk in its orbit; the lines of the face strongly marked: a hooked nose, a thick lower lip; an expression of anxiety or fear—a false smile. The miser often stoops, being constantly at the desk or little given to bodily exercise. His walk is noiseless, his steps are short, his hands betray nervousness and anxiety—eager to receive, slow to give. The successful issue of a transaction will cause a cynical expression of satisfaction on his countenance. His sense of economy keeps him in an abject state of penury—he punishes his body to pamper his purse, and deprives himself of the necessaries of life. He always pleads poverty. He is essentially selfish, and often cruel—most times cowardly, always plodding and deceitful. Like ambition, this passion is never satisfied (Fig. 39, Chap. XI., page 104).

VII. SELFISHNESS.—Intense love of life causes the selfish man to sacrifice everything to his desires. Intense love of money causes the miser to sacrifice all for the gratification of his passion. The former never denies himself anything: the latter, never indulges in anything. The one sleeps soundly, the other is kept awake by his constant fears. The selfish man loves himself beyond everything and everybody; the miser loves his money better than himself. The one thinks of the present, the other of the future. The first creates for himself endless wants, the second endless perplexities. The contempt for others is the only thing they possess in common.

This sentiment can only be expressed by an utter disregard of anything that does not affect our interest. The misfortunes or happiness of others do not concern the selfish man—his own personality being his first consideration, he never wins others' sympathy. In society, he monopolises the conversation; pays little or no attention to others. Never susceptible of a kind impulsive emotion, his face reflects the indifference of his heart. No softness, no kindness, in his features; cynical in his observations; never compassionate for others; indifferent to the pain he may cause to others by his indiscreet questions, if it gratifies his morbid sense of curiosity. The actions expressive of this sentiment would be more calm than boisterous, as the selfish man does not like to put himself out of the way.

VIII. INGRATITUDE—This degraded feeling is the result of selfishness and often of vanity.

When success or fortune smiles upon us, we are apt to forget those who by their kindness helped us through our misfortunes. We stifle all kind sentiments towards our benefactors: either we cannot bear the idea that we owe our position to them, and not to our talent alone; or the fear of having to repay past kindness by favours or money makes us overlook the past. Ingratitude assumes the same expressions as selfishness.

IX. ENVY.—Envy is a passion which we carefully hide from others, as it is a degrading disposition of our nature. Incapacity is its direct cause. Our pride suffers in witnessing the superiority of others. We become envious of those we vainly endeavour to imitate. Their success, their eminent qualities, cause in us an irrepressible sense of grief and disappointment. It is an intense desire to possess what we see in others. The envious man is incapable of hiding his feelings, his countenance betrays the agony of his soul. If he hears of his rival's good fortune, or hears him praised, he changes colour and turns pale: envy rushes to his features, he tries to check the enthusiasm by throwing out such insinuations as may prejudice him in others' estimation. Envy works in the dark, and covers itself with the garment of hypocrisy. We often bestow praises and flatteries on our rivals, and assure them of our kindly feelings, whilst in our hearts we loathe them. Eminent men are the victims of envy; and if calumny does not arrest their ascending star, we oppose to them men of inferior capacity on whom we lavish unlimited praise. The envious man has not a moment of rest. All his plotting against others' success or happiness does not afford a single instant of satisfaction. A false look and restless action would express this passion.

X. AMBITION.—This passion is caused by an intense desire to obtain eminence. It is an incessant domineering eager feeling that urges us on towards the object we may have in view. Emulation, envy, are the promoters of ambition. The ambitious man loves praise and admiration ; he is generally selfish, and capable of all the passions that may serve his purpose—his desires are un-limited—his activity never ceases ; rest and sleep rarely comfort his anxious mind. Impatient and anxious at all times, his move-ments are rapid and abrupt, his features restless, his physiognomy betrays incessant preoccupation. Constant thought of the future fills his soul with perplexity ; hope tortures him, whereas it comforts other men.

# CHAPTER XIV.

## ANALYSIS OF FAVOURABLE SENTIMENTS.

I. CALMNESS.—Perfect symmetry in the features, such as we see in Fig. 1, Chap. XI., page 87, reflects a quiet state of the mind. Repose in the attitude and movements are indicative of the harmony existing in the thoughts, and a passive state of the soul.

II. ADMIRATION.—Admiration is, after repose, the most temperate sentiment of the soul. The features of the face, as we see in Fig. 5, Chap. XI., page 88, are slightly raised, and in a symmetrical manner. The eyes and eyebrows assume a more elevated position whilst the mouth opens. The action of the latter can be explained by the fact that as soon as our sentiments acquire some degree of intensity, the action of the heart quickens, the breathing becomes more rapid and necessitates a greater amount of air, which is obtained by opening the mouth.

III. ASTONISHMENT—SURPRISE. Astonishment differs from admiration inasmuch as its features are more characteristic; the mouth is more open, the eyes more fixed, the eyebrows more elevated, and the breathing less free; the respiration even stops suddenly and the thoughts are arrested at the sight of some striking object that presents itself before our sight, Fig. 6, Chap. XI., page 88. A success contrary to our expectation, a happy and unexpected event, causes an astonishment which betrays itself by a smile. If this sentiment is the result of some extraordinary fact, either absurd or otherwise, the expression of astonishment will be accompanied by the following actions. We throw our head and body slightly back, we raise our hands quickly and symmetrically; this last action being the result of the rapid passage from one sentiment to the other. We often see people stopping short in the middle of their work at the sight of some object which attracts their eyes. This expression becomes that of a man who, on hearing some extraordinary intelligence, is filled with astonishment. We remember seeing a blacksmith, whose entire attention was so thoroughly arrested that he forgot to strike the iron whilst it was hot. This sense of astonishment is but of short duration, and turns almost immediately into either doubt, disgust, fear, terror, &c.

IV. JOY. — When our imagination is filled with pleasant thoughts, our countenance assumes an expression of serenity and satisfaction, Fig. 2, Chap. XI., page 87. When great events enhance this happy disposition, our features acquire a greater degree of expression—that of joy. A frank and open appearance is the unmistakable sign of this sentiment. The forehead is serene, free from traces of care : the head gracefully elevated, the eyes bright, the mouth smiling : the hands and arms kept away from the body. The walk is lively : grace, suppleness, lightness and harmony in the movements, and in all the limbs, are the characteristic features of a happy mind. These movements are subject to modifications, according to the cause that prompts them.

The joy of the proud man who sees the happy issue of his ambitious plans will cause a general expression of self-complacency; his face will betray satisfaction, his movements will be free and unconstrained. If great ideas occupy his mind his countenance will no longer bear the expression of pure joy, but it will assume a look of joy mixed with pride.

The lover whose soul nourishes rapturously beautiful and sweet ideas betrays his sentiments by a spontaneous pure joy.

V. RAPTUROUS JOY.—The sentiment of joy, as well as its expression, is susceptible of great modification. The highest degree of joy or rapture is only a strengthening of the above features, which entirely lose their grace—if they do not disappear altogether—the moment joy becomes noisy and exuberant, and degenerates into such petulance as to cause contortions of the face, and turn the free and graceful movements of the body into the gesticulations of a clown.

This sentiment seems to electrify all our senses, which assume extraordinary activity when under its influence. Banqueting, singing, dancing, laughing, clapping of the hands, a desire to communicate with those whom we wish to share our happiness, kissing, embracing, shaking hands, protestations of friendship, spontaneous movements of generosity, tears of joy, are all signs of an exuberance of feeling in our soul.

Milton, in "l'Allegro," portrays the expression of the sentiment of joy : —

> " Haste thee, nymph, and bring with thee
> Jest and youthful jollity ;
> Quips and cranks, and wanton wiles,
> Nods, and winks, and wreathed smiles,
> Such as hang on Hebe's cheek
> And love to live in dimple sleek :
> Sport that wrinkled Care derides,
> And Laughter holding both his sides ;
> Come, and trip it as you go
> On the light fantastic toe."

Rapture may be expressed by signs and tokens totally different from those already described.

Quiet rapture may be indicated by the reclining attitude of the body, the limbs drooping by their own weight, the languishing expression of the face—the eyes shut, so that nothing should disturb the mind from its contemplation, and the happy expression of the mouth which betrays a smile are the signs of a person who concentrates the entire soul on some imaginary object, and also of joy, such as we often see in gentle and sentimental natures.

When this sentiment assumes this form we seek solitary places, where the quaint scenery corresponds to the happy state of our mind.

VI. SENSITIVENESS.—This sentiment is caused by a certain weakness of the nervous system, and betrays itself by an expression of melancholy or grief—the sight of others' misfortunes, the sound of music, the contemplation of a touching picture, affects our sensibility and makes us shed tears, causing at the same time a nervous and irregular course of action, which reflects the state of our mind.

VII. MELANCHOLY.—Collins well describes the expression of this feeling :—

> " With eyes upraised, as one inspired,
> Pale Melancholy sat retired,
> And from her wild sequestered seat,
> In notes by distance made more sweet,
> Poured through the mellow horn her pensive soul.
> \*    \*    \*    \*    \*    \*
> Round a holy calm diffusing
> Love of peace and lonely musing."

VIII. HOPE.—Man is the only living being susceptible of hope ; happy when full of it, he weeps when he has lost it. None but he conceives joy at the thought of the causes that might realise the possession of a desired object. There exists no reality in the sensation we feel ; it is always in the future we lay the foundation of our happiness.

> " Hope bade the lovely scenes at distance hail."—*Collins*.

Painters represent it as the smiling goddess, who shows herself constantly before the eyes of the unfortunate, rich or poor ; we all conceive plans which we hope to realise. To hope is to be happy. The ruined man hopes to retrieve his fortune. Hope is the most favourable sentiment for the equilibrium and harmony of human feelings ; the whole of the nervous system is put into action by it.

Hope is a compound passion. Fear accompanies it, as though to check its impulses. Despondency generally succeeds to disappointed hope. Fig. 8, Chap. XI., page 89, is a true expression of this sentiment. The eyes betray great eagerness, whilst the eyebrows, being slightly arched, express doubt or fear. The mouth shows, by its smiling expression, the active part it takes in the anticipated success of the future. Fig. 7, Chap. XI., page 89, which is that of eagerness, expresses eagerness and sensuality. Fig. 8, which is that of hope, expresses eagerness and fear. One thinks of the present, the other of the future.

# CHAPTER XV.

I. LOVE :—AFFECTION IN ITS VARIOUS PHASES.
—Edmund Burke, in his essays on the sublime and
beautiful has some valuable remarks on the outward expression of
the feeling of love. He says—"When we have before us such
objects as excite love and complacency, the body is affected, so
far as I could observe, much in the following manner :—The head
reclines something on one side ; the eyelids are more closed than
usual ; the eyes roll gently, with an inclination to the object ; the
mouth is a little opened, and the breath drawn slowly, with now and
then a low sigh. The whole body is composed, and the hands fall
idly to the sides. All this is accompanied with an inward sense
of melting and languor. These appearances are always proportioned to the degree of beauty in the object and of sensibility in
the observer. And this gradation from the highest pitch of
beauty and sensibility, even to the lowest of mediocrity and indifference, and their correspondent effects ought to be kept in view ;
else this description will seem exaggerated, which certainly is
not—

> ' Man sees in woman the companion of his life, who shares his
> sorrows and happiness.'

In refined natures love is an enthusiastic contemplation of eternal beauty. It becomes a dream of perfection, and a pursuit of the ideal which rallies heaven and earth. Love being the most acute sentiment of our soul, is susceptible of all the violent passions that move humanity."

II. Esteem.—Esteem is a temperate sentiment, prompted by a sense of dignity and admiration. A man who acts uprightly never loses himself in his own estimation. If we admire certain qualities in others, we esteem the persons in whom we recognise them. The expression of this sentiment, as we see in Fig. 3, Chap. XI., reflects the state of the soul, scarcely disturbed by a calm emotion, the eyes only assuming a slightly greater intensity in the expression. This, like all moderate feelings, belongs to a calm, reflective mind, and is expressed by actions of a similar kind, such as a cordial putting forth of the hand, a general appearance of welcome, &c.

III. Sympathy.—Sympathy is a spontaneous movement of the soul, which is caused by the admiration we may have for others. It is the first step towards friendship and love. It is also an impulsive movement of a tender heart, and often takes the form of compassion, pity. The expression of sympathy can only be rendered by attitudes or actions suitable to either of the above sentiments.

IV. Friendship.—This sentiment is the result of admiration, esteem, and sympathy, and is susceptible of many gradations. Considered in its abstract sense, it is a noble feeling rising to the greatest devotion. We love a true friend, and for him we are ready to make the greatest sacrifices. In him we place the most implicit confidence. We admire his qualities, and overlook his faults. The desire to communicate with a friend, the pleasure we experience in his company, are expressed by our attitude, which betrays a sense of infinite complacency and enjoyment. Embracing, kissing, shaking of hands, rapidity of expression in the discourse, are the features and actions suitable to this sentiment.

The expression of friendship assumes a more or less demonstrative form according to our disposition. Reserved natures rarely show their feelings, and are generally very sparing of demon-

strations.  Impulsive natures, on the contrary, have an uncontrollable exuberance of expression.  In this case the action often
assumes a compound form :

FIG. 49.

In Fig. 49 we see an attitude expressing joy, eagerness and doubt,
such as that of a person unexpectedly meeting a beloved friend :
the body thrown back expresses doubt, the face joy, and the hands

K

warmly extended show eagerness. The rapid succession of these sentiments would correspond to the emotions we should feel at seeing a friend we thought dead or lost to us. Great effect may be derived on the stage from such a situation, which is highly impressive. This feeling of doubt succeeded by joy is well depicted by Campbell in the meeting of the Oneida Chief with his friend in "Gertrude of Wyoming":—

> "Nor could the group a smile control,
> The long and doubtful scrutiny to view;
> At length delight o'er all his features stole—
> 'It is—my own!' he cried, and clasped him to his soul."

If instead of rushing at once into the friend's arms, a well-timed moment of suspense or doubt is observed, the feeling of the spectator gradually works up to a climax, until it reaches its highest degree of intensity, when the actor acceding to the impulse of nature, throws himself on the bosom of his friend, and by the sublimity of his actions electrifies the public.

V. PATERNAL LOVE.—Paternal love is not only the most noble sentiment of a generous heart, but the sweetest pleasure for a sensitive man. It consoles us for the irksomeness of advancing age. A father lives again in his children. "And I go courting in my boys," says the poet.

In the IV. Act of "King Lear," when the unhappy king sees his daughter Cordelia, his emotion is so great that he scarcely believes his senses, and says in his anguish:—

"Pray do not mock me: I am a very foolish, fond old man, fourscore and upward, not an hour more or less: and, to deal plainly, I fear I am not in my perfect mind. Do not laugh at me! for as I am a man, I think this lady to be my child, Cordelia."

Although weakened by age, suffering, and mental torture, although his sight is dim, yet the heart of the most unfortunate of kings and of fathers has recognised his child. How he presses her to his bosom, kisses her, smooths her hair so as to remove all obstacles that might conceal her from his sight! His solicitude, his caresses, his tears of joy, are the expressions of his entire soul. Such sentiments are so natural that they seem simple and easy to represent; and yet it requires the sensitiveness and heart of a great artist to render them in their true purity.

VII. MATERNAL LOVE.—Maternal love is the most tender sentiment in living nature. It is the sweetest and most generous movement which the natural instinct can possibly prompt. It is the first inclination in animal economy. The savage woman watches over and tends her child; she carries it on her back. No human being is destitute of this inclination. Animals themselves carefully watch over their little ones. The sentiments of a mother are all spontaneous, never reflective or calculating.

James Montgomery, the poet, has eloquently expressed the nature of this feeling in his exquisite poem, entitled, "A Mother's Love."

> " To bring a helpless babe to light,
>    Then, while it lies forlorn,
> To gaze upon that dearest sight,
>    And feel herself new born ;
> In its existence lose her own,
> And live and breathe in it alone ;
>    This is a mother's love."

VII. VENERATION.—This sentiment is caused by the love and admiration we have for a moral being whose age, experience, superiority, impresses us with respect. It is a kind sentiment of the heart, which is the very opposite of pride, not only in its very nature, but also in the attitude and action it suggests. Both these sentiments are expressed by the same metaphor. Haughtiness is the result of pride—humility, that of veneration. The entire frame in this latter sentiment assumes such an expression as we see in Fig. 4, Chap. XI. The muscles of the face cease to act with their wonted vigour—the eyebrows, the cheeks, the mouth, incline slightly downwards when this sentiment is inspired by respect, or the features assume an expression of tenderness, as in Fig. 50, when it is inspired by love. In both instances, the face has a kind of intense look, which gives it an appearance of sadness and melancholy.

FIG. 50.

VIII. FILIAL LOVE.—This kind of affection is a feeling which most needs the help of virtue to remain constant. It is partly founded on gratitude, which is but in itself a fugitive and passing sentiment, which requires all the strength of principle, if it is to prove lasting. Filial piety is more an acquired virtue than an uncontrollable impulse of nature. It exists but to a small degree in animals, and is strongly developed in man by the kindness of a father and mother. This sentiment is the result of love and veneration, and is a noble feeling, leading to the greatest devotion.

> " My Father, shall the joyous throng
> Swell high for me the bridal song?
> Shall the gay nuptial board be spread—
> The festal garland bind my head—

And thou in grief, in peril roam,
And make the wilderness thy home ?
No ! I am here, with thee to share
All suffering mortal strength may bear !
And oh ! whate'er thy foes decree
In life, in death, in chains, or free,
Well, well, I feel in thee secure —
Thy heart and hand alike are pure."
(*A Tale of the Secret Tribunal*—MRS HEMANS.)

IX. HUMILITY.—This sentiment is natural, and shows itself when we find ourselves in the presence of those whose power and superiority make us feel our weakness and inferiority. The fear that they should discover our deficiencies causes an irrepressible sense of shyness or diffidence. We feel that we are unworthy of their society. We humble ourselves when we are conscious of our weakness, or when we address our superiors on whom depends our position in life. This sentiment is also prompted by our religious feelings. It is finely expressed in the words of Portia to Bassanio, who is to be her husband, when, in her humility, she describes herself as

" An unlessoned girl, unskilled, unpracticed ;
Happy in this, she is not yet so old,
But she may learn ; happier in this,
She is not bred so dull but she can learn ;
Happiest of all is, that her gentle spirit
Commits itself to yours to be directed,
As from her lord, her governor, her king."

X. DEVOTION.—Veneration and humility are the promoters of this sentiment. When we worship, we venerate the greatness of the Creator and humble ourselves before Him. In doing so we raise our eyes towards heaven, and join our hands, and bend our knees as in prayer. The expression of this passion is rendered by a combination of contrary actions. The hands are raised to the breast, the eyes towards heaven, whilst the other features of the face, as well as the limbs of the body, have a tendency downwards. The actions of the hand show the intense feeling of the soul, whilst the eyes turn upwards in supplication, in *hope* of forgiveness or succour. If this feeling becomes the predominant passion of our soul, the expression of the face loses its vivacity and becomes sad. The constant preoccupation with the same idea, which is purely imaginative, and which neither the mind nor the senses can possibly realise, causes a disturbance in the being which nothing can remove. Carried to excess, devotion becomes fanaticism, and assumes all the disorderly features of madness. We see that the Egyptians, in their frenzy, throw themselves under the hoofs of the horse that carries their priest; others punish themselves by tearing their flesh, and showing all the outward signs of insanity.

Although a devotional person may feel perfectly happy, yet the expression of the attitude is that of dejection. The eyes become dull, and reflect an inward and mystic preoccupation, an imagination that broods secretly over exalted ideas.

XI. BENEVOLENCE.—The expression of this sentiment must assume the appearance of friendship in its more reserved form. Kind sentiments towards our fellow-creatures, encouraging words, accompanied by a gentle pat of the hand on the shoulders, or on the head, if to a child, are the characteristic signs of benevolence.

XII. MODESTY.—This sentiment resembles humility or veneration, inasmuch as the attitude and manners are unassuming; but it springs from a different cause. A modest man is diffident of his own powers, and ready at all times to acknowledge those of others. For this reason it is the very opposite of presumption. This sentiment is generally the graceful attribute of a kind nature and of a great mind. Selfishness, or pride, would clash with modesty; Fig. 51.

XIII. PITY.—This sentiment is prompted by a sense of sympathy directed with more or less energy towards those who suffer. It is a spontaneous movement of the soul. Reflection rarely takes part in this kind of sentiment—when we give to a poor man we do not calculate what use he will make of our gift. It is expressed by tears, especially when we sympathise with moral

FIG. 51.

suffering. The idea of pity is finely expressed in Goldsmith's "Deserted Village," among the attributes of the good country clergyman :—

> " Pleased with his guests, the good man learned to glow,
> And quite forgot their vices in their woe—
> Careless their merits or their faults to scan,
> His pity gave ere charity began."

# CHAPTER XVI.

### ANALYSIS OF UNFAVOURABLE SENTIMENTS.

I. AVERSION.—Passions are among the most striking phenomena of our sensitive nature. Our activity is set in motion by our sensitiveness and intelligence, and obeys either a mechanical impression, or an instinctive appetite, arising out of our physical cravings, or an intellectual direction, guided by reason and ideas. All unsatisfied desires cause in us a painful sentiment or suffering. On the contrary, when we satisfy our cravings or desires, we derive a sense of pleasure and contentment. Simultaneously with the painful sentiment caused in us by our unsatisfied wants is produced a tendency towards the objects which we wish to obtain; and the same reason that makes us pursue with avidity everything that would gratify and give pleasure, makes us fly with the same eagerness from anything that may cause pain or suffering.

This latter sentiment is called *Aversion.*

When eagerness is increased by long expectation, or crossed by obstacles, it acquires a certain intensity and becomes *passion.* Passion, therefore, is craving, or aversion carried to its highest degree of force. These two passions, which are the moving power of our sensitiveness, the double movement which causes us to run after pleasure, or fly from suffering, correspond to the two phenomena, called by physiologists movement of expansion and movement of contraction, and by analogy give rise to the sympathetic, or sociable passions, and the passions that can be called, on the other hand selfish, or anti-sociable.

This passion assumes the form of repugnance—contempt, hatred, fear, &c., and is rendered by the features belonging to any one of them. Its cause may be moral or physical, and is suggested by the painful impression that may either affect our senses or our mind.

II. REPUGNANCE.—This sentiment is caused by the painful impression made by some object on our senses. If our eyes are affected, we naturally shut them, or hide them with our hand, or turn our head away. The features of our physiognomy become more or less distorted. Repugnance at outward objects we express by turning up our nose, the mouth following the same direction, thus causing the eyebrows to lower themselves.

III. DECEPTION.—A feeling of disappointment is caused by the deception we meet with in life. Disappointments of the heart through deception are the most cruel. We enter our career full of hope, of illusions. We believe in others, because we are loyal and generous, but soon we are taught the error of our impressions. From being deceived we become deceivers; deceptions throw bitterness and disgust on our existence, and although our reason struggles against the sorrow they cause, yet time never entirely repairs their everlasting havoc. We depart from the path of virtue; and from being children of nature, we become men of the world. The expressions and actions belonging to this sentiment would be the same as those of sorrow. A disappointed man has a careworn appearance. Smiles and happiness have forsaken his countenance. We naturally turn away from a person who deceives our expectations, or refuses a favour, and our disappointment turns either to grief, anger, or contempt.

IV. CONTEMPT.—This sentiment, in its general acceptation, is the sentence rendered by public conscience, against the man who has forfeited public respect. It is a just punishment upon him whose actions are no longer worthy of esteem and favourable regard. This sentiment, shows by its very signification that it ought not to be indulged indiscriminately,—and yet we see people in society assume airs of contempt, on the strength of their rank, fortune, birth, or other adventitious advantages. It is the sentiment of contempt that causes hatred in those against whom it is directed. Pride, vanity, selfishness, are therefore the promoters of this passion, which assumes their different expression and attitudes. If this passion is provoked by an insult received from a person whom we consider to be our inferior, it will be expressed by the dignity of our attitude—a severe look directed up and down towards the person, a sneering smile on the face, a slight shrugging of the shoulders, are signs denoting our superiority over those who have excited our contempt. Although this passion and pride are expressed by metaphoric actions, yet they differ entirely in their meaning. Pride is the result of the excellent opinion we have of ourselves; contempt, of the poor opinion we have of others. There are many actions and expressions to render this passion. The body turned sideways, a careless glance over the shoulder, or throwing a proud and hasty look, as though the object or persons were unworthy of closer examination. We cast away from us objects belonging to those we despise. Othello throws money at Emilia's feet when he says—" There's money for your pains."

Neglecting those who are present, or showing them indifference, such as pretending to forget their presence by paying attention to others—whistling or humming whilst they are asking pressing questions—laughing or sneering at their distress, or keeping people waiting in the ante-room, are all typical expressions of this feeling.

V. SARCASM.—This form of satire springs from an unkind disposition in our nature which prompts us to take advantage of our natural gifts to turn others into ridicule, sparing neither their natural defects, their afflictions or misfortunes, nor their feelings of humiliation or injury. It is also the weapon of the weak against the strong. A man gifted with a noble nature or great physical strength is rarely sarcastic. The indulgence of this sentiment is often the result of the confidence we feel in our natural wit, and therefore is not devoid of vanity or pride. In turning others into ridicule, not only do we derive a certain satisfaction at causing a laugh, which is invariably provoked at their expense, but we gratify our selfish pride and vanity by showing the contrast between their deficiencies and our own capacities. Sarcasm is the vindictive proceeding of a man who by natural incapacity, or by his humble position, cannot cope with others. Envy and presumption are at the bottom of this uncharitable propensity. To throw ridicule on others is to boast of our own excellence. A sneering smile, great activity of movement in the eyebrows, as well as a malicious expression in the eyes, are the principal outward signs of sarcasm.

VI. HYPOCRISY.—This passion hides itself under the cloak of kind sentiments. Cowardice, villainy are its main springs. It is a prying propensity of the soul, a plodding perseverance that works in the dark to undo others. Hypocrisy has been aptly called the homage that vice renders to virtue. Beware of the false man who greets you with a smile or assures you of his kind feelings, for if you make a confidant of him he will turn his knowledge to his own benefit at the cost of your interest and good fame. Iago is the true type of the hypocritical false man. Slander, false and calumnious insinuations are his hidden weapons. Envy, selfishness have a great part in this passion. Although the hypocrite assumes a soft persuasive tone of voice and has a smile on his lips, yet his attitude does not inspire confidence; for notwithstanding his art at concealing his feelings, the state of his soul is reflected in his features, which assume a restless and deceitful expression. The face of the hypocrite is often pale: he never looks others in the face, he seems to be afraid of their searching glance; his manners are calculated and insinuating; he rarely makes an impetuous movement,—his walk is silent, almost mysterious; his action uncertain, his attitude humble, so as never to raise suspicion. Friendly and sympathising in appearance, false and treacherous in reality. Hypocrisy frequently hides itself under the cloak of religion, and although indulgent towards the greatest sinners, even the most charitable man is averse to hypocrites. The author of the *Henriade* has well said:—

> "La tendre hypocrisie a l'air plein de douceur,
> Le ciel est dans ses yeux, l'enfer est dans son cœur."

VII. JEALOUSY AND ENVY.—Jealousy is a passion that causes a painful and uncertain struggle between anger and overwhelming suffering; doubt, suspicion, revenge, despair, alternate in the soul of the jealous man. Cupidity or ambition may be the cause of this sentiment, which in this case assumes the form of selfishness and envy. For instance, the success of others who follow the same pursuit as ours, causes in us a feeling of grief and annoyance which we cannot repress. If they fail, we rejoice at their misfortune, although it may be of no benefit to us. When our soul is tortured by this passion, our features lose their harmonious and kind expression, assuming that of hatred and craft. If love is the main spring of this passion, its features assume a striking variety of expression. Some define jealousy as being a restless state of the soul, which causes in us an eager desire to possess the glory, happiness, and talent of others. Some attribute this definition to envy. This difference, however, may be established between envy and jealousy : we envy what others possess, we are jealous of what we possess. If we accept this distinction as being the correct one, we may say that jealousy has, morally speaking, no other special acceptation, except inasmuch as it serves to designate the morbid affection of the heart, the principal cause of which is the suffering of unhappy love.

Our imagination creates a thousand causes for apprehension ; we become uneasy, restless, irritable ; when in the presence of our love we lose all control over our feelings ; we give offence when we ought to show kindness and give comfort ; we quarrel, we become passionate, we turn pale, our heart beats violently, our features become distorted, our breathing is heavy—and yet amidst this storm of passions, we are ready to cry, to beg, to implore forgiveness, to repent the injustice of our suspicions, doubts, and accusa tions. In the character of Faulkland, in "*The Rivals*," we have a good delineation of jealousy. This fierce and disorderly passion often leads to the most deplorable extremes. If jealousy does not take the violent form which we see in Othello, even in its milder expression it is selfish, unreasonable, exacting—a harassing feeling. Othello, blinded by his frenzy, murders the loving and virtuous Desdemona, who cannot restore the peace of his mind by her true and touching protestations of love and innocence. Faulkland tortures the heart of his gentle mistress by his incessant doubts and suspicions. Jealousy is a disorderly passion, susceptible of an infinite variety of expression.

Sheridan describes jealous love by the following lines in his opera of "*The Duenna*":—

> "Though cause for suspicion appears,
>     Yet proofs of her love, too, are strong;
> I'm a wretch if I'm right in my fears,
>     And unworthy of bliss if I'm wrong.
> What heart-breaking torments from jealousy flow,
> Ah! none but the jealous—the jealous can know!
>
> When blest with the smiles of my fair,
>     I know not how much I adore;
> Those smiles if another but share,
>     And I wonder I prized them no more!
> Then whence can I hope a relief from my woe,
> When the farther she seems, still the fonder I grow?"

We may conclude that the disorderly passion shows its gradations from mere teasing to murder—some it renders criminals, others odious, others simply ridiculous.

VIII. HATRED AND THE KINDRED PASSIONS.—Hatred is a passion that implies the idea of hostility towards others. J. J. Rousseau describes it as a manifest intention to do injury. It is fiery, stubborn, blind, unjust. It tortures the heart, and is spiteful against others, whose very virtues it blackens. It is generally more open and outspoken than rancour. Hatred is caused by certain proceedings that hurt us in our affections, in the most sensitive parts of our souls. Animosity springs from more remote causes : such as may exist between two persons violently opposed in their political opinions. We may say that *Antipathy* is a want of harmony between ourselves and a person or a thing, who is, as it were, of a different nature to ourselves, and is caused by incompatibility of humour.

Aversion differs from hatred by its greater violence, and more resembles horror.

Disgust is more passive, being akin to *ennui.*

Repugnance is more active, and springs more from rebellion.

Figs. 35, 37, and 38, pages 71 and 73, are expressive of this passion, and reflect by the irregularity of the lines, and the expression of the eyes and mouth the disorderly state of the soul.

This passion belongs to an essentially vigorous mind ; a timid or apathetic nature is rarely troubled with such violent sentiments ; the actions and attitudes would therefore follow its gradations, which assume the forms belonging to the passions illustrated in the plates on physiognomy.

IX. VENGEANCE. — The desire for vengeance is a terrible passion that knows no bounds. It is a fire that consumes the soul, and is not easily extinguished in the heart of man. If it cannot give vent to its rage on the desired person, it falls on persons, or on things that may have an interest in or belong to him. If it cannot attack these objects, it seizes the first person or thing that happens to be in its way, and quite innocent objects, beaten, trampled, smashed, torn, experience all the fury of this frantic passion. If our vengeance dares not, or cannot be satisfied in this way, it uses violence against itself. We bite our lips, our flesh—we tear our hair, and show every sign of rage and desperation. When in the fifth act, the unfortunate messenger tells Macbeth, " Methought the wood began to move ! " Macbeth seizes him by the throat and roars out "Liar and slave ! " thus giving way to his passion for revenge—he vents his fury on an innocent man, unable as he is to refrain from such an act of violence. There are other symptoms belonging to this fierce passion, very different in their aspect, although not less cruel in their effect. A cowardly man, who indulges in the lust of revenge, gives way to its cravings in an indirect manner. Instead of anger, rage, despair, his attitudes are calm; he hides his dark purposes under the false appearance of a bitter smile. His expression is cynical, his looks are false, his manner soft, unctuous, his step is noiseless. He resorts to calumny and false insinuations. He is plodding, persevering, jesuitical, hypocritical. He is too cowardly to take his own revenge himself, but takes advantage of others' weaknesses to excite in them his own sentiments. Iago is the true impersonation of this detestable feeling. His jealousy leads him to his revenge, which he accomplishes without noise; and his hypocrisy is such that he is called "honest Iago" by his very victims. This passion can only be rendered by expressions belonging to contempt, rage, hatred.

X. ANGER, RAGE, &c.—This passion is rendered by the same expressions as vengeance, or by such attitudes as we see in Figs. 40 and 41, pages 75 and 76, or in Chap. XI. An angry man threatens to punish or to strike. His features assume a severe, if not a hard expression. Want of due regard from others, or contempt on their part, especially from those we love, will cause this disorder in our soul. Anger, raised to its highest pitch, assumes a more violent form, and becomes rage. The first symptoms, previous to an outburst of passion, betray themselves by the pallor of our faces and the contraction of our features. We frown; our eyes assume a fierce expression, we bite our lips; our movements become agitated and abrupt. If we speak, our lips quiver; we stutter forth our words, we breathe with difficulty, our hands become restless; the whole of our nervous system seems shaken by the force of our passion. In the next stage of this passion all the moral and physical faculties given us by nature come out, and become, as it were, intensified. All the muscles of the body acquire a convulsive power. The eyes become fiery, and roll in their orbits. The hands contract violently, the mouth foams, the teeth grind fiercely. The whole body, equally with the soul, is in convulsions. The veins of the neck and temples swell; the blood rushes to the face; the movements are violent. The stride is long, heavy, and irregular. We stamp the ground with our feet, we tear our hair, we gesticulate furiously, we walk to and fro with frantic impetuosity, we cry, we shout, we laugh hysterically; we smash everything we get in our hands—in short, an enraged person offers the dismal spectacle of a man who has lost control over himself.

XI. DESPAIR.—Taken in its literal meaning, this word expresses the utter loss of hope: according to the usual acceptation, it means intense grief. In the first case, despair is a permanent, and an almost incurable state. In the second case it is a state of passing crisis—the very violence of which guarantees its short duration. This passion assumes different attitudes and expressions. When it has become the normal state of our nature, it causes a moral obduracy, a strong condition of insensibility which renders us indifferent to all that passes around. A pallid face, a haggard, vacant look, sadness stamped on our features—tears, sighs, desponding attitudes, such as drooping of the head and wringing of the hands, are the expressive features of this sentiment: the outward signs of a soul tortured and haunted by the intense grief of despair—such as a mother would feel after the loss of a beloved child. If it is the cause of a passing crisis, its expression assumes a violent form, and can only be rendered by attitudes and actions suggestive of great passions. The violent despair of a mother over the corpse of her child is one that betrays the intensity of grief by an outburst of tears, she throws herself into imploring attitudes, wringing her hands with force. The remorse of a lover, who gives way to his repentance, is shown by violent gestures. Thus, Othello, in the paroxysm of his grief, commits suicide to liberate himself from the agony of his soul. All these outward signs are similar to the expression of rage and anger, although prompted by very different causes. See Chap. XI., also Fig. 45, page 80.

XII. FEAR, TERROR.—This sentiment is the result of a shock received by our nervous system, caused by the consciousness of danger. It affects our mental faculties to such a degree that we lose all control over ourselves; our countenance, our actions and attitudes, all combine in reflecting the disordered state of our mind. The lines of our faces become distorted, the look haggard and fearful, the eyebrows strongly arched; we tremble from head to foot, our breathing becomes spasmodic, our hearts beat rapidly. If we have enough strength left, we run in frantic terror; we shout; we scream—such are the signs of this disorderly sentiment.

Considered under their different aspects, fear and terror are expressed by a variety of actions, some of which it is important to enumerate. The fear of ill-treatment causes a series of expressions such as these. We protest, supplicate, promise. We tremble, our hands try to protect the body from apprehended blows, we fall on our knees, we cry; we shout. In one word, the soul discharges its burden by demonstrative action. We crouch and cover our ears and faces with our hands if we fear the report of thunder. We cover our eyes to avoid the sight of lightning. Cain, flying from his victim, and fearing the voice of God, instinctively protects his body with his arms (Fig. 44, page 79), and looks up in terror. The sight of a serpent would cause us to look back in the midst of our flight. Rarely do we fly from an object, real or imaginary, without turning back to see if it follows us. Danger acts on our weakened nerves with a paralysing effect. It fascinates us; we become powerless.

If this sentiment is caused by the disturbed state of our conscience, our imagination becomes the prey of horrible fancies, which throw disorder and TERROR into our inmost feelings.

Macbeth, in Scene IV., Act III., being invited by the lords of his court to occupy the vacant place at the banquet table, says: "The table's full!" Lennox answers: "Here's a place reserved, sir." Macb.: "Where?" Lennox: "There, my good lord. What is't that moves your highness?" Macb.: "Which of you has done this?"—Macbeth has just perceived the ghost of Banquo sitting in the vacant chair. At the sight of this unhappy victim he becomes livid with terror; his eyes are starting out of their orbits; his breath stops short; his features become distorted. He raises his trembling hands towards Banquo's spectre, the fingers stretched forth in agony. The

L

sight is so terrible that the hands withdraw instinctively and cover
the face of the man, who can no longer stand against the terror it
inspires.   He then staggers back and falls on one knee, one
hand seizing the first object it meets that offers a support to his
body, whilst the other hand stretches again towards the vision,
as though to keep it off.   In this attitude he says, with a voice
stifled with fear :

> " Thou canst not say I did it ! "

When the ghost reappears, Macbeth says (Fig. 42, page 77) :

> "Avaunt, and quit my sight !
> Let the earth hide thee.
> Thy bones are marrowless, thy blood is cold ;
> Thou hast no speculation in those eyes
> Which thou dost glare with."

Macbeth says to his wife, who, after rebuking him, asks him
indignantly : "Are you a man ? "   "Ay, and a bold one, that
dare to look on that which might appal the devil."   We may
imagine how strong must the effects of terror be, if a man
possessing such a courage as Macbeth succumbs under it.   To
render such a scene with effect, the actor must be gifted with a
vigorous temperament.   Although he may have full control over
himself in ordinary life, yet his nature must be sensitive and alive
to strong passions ; a placid and indifferent mind will never
grasp the powerful sentiments required to act the part of Macbeth.
An actor destitute of these qualifications must resort to artificial
means ; his actions and diction will be overstrained, and impress
the public with a painful sense of his useless efforts.

XIII. REPENTANCE.—This sentiment is the result of sorrow
for wrong-doing.   A well balanced mind feels grieved at having
said some hasty word or done some action which may have
given offence or caused prejudice.   The expression of this
sentiment would be the same as in sorrow.   The attitude of
repentance is that of humility.   We humble ourselves before
those we have offended.   Tears stream down our cheeks, without
our being able to repress them ; and we do not recover our
sense of comfort and satisfaction until we have obtained forgive-

ness. Signs of fear are also perceptible in this sentiment, as we not only feel always reluctant to ask others for their pardon, but we fear that they may resent our offence and treat us with severity. The expression of shame is also one of the features of this sentiment.

XIV. REMORSE.—This passion is the result of a terror-stricken conscience—it is a darker kind of repentance. The murderer is haunted by the visage of his victim. He sees blood wherever he goes; his guilt terrifies him. A look from others is an accusation; an unexpected noise startles him. His conscience scourges him day and night. The money he may have gained by his crime burns his fingers; he does not know what to do with it for fear of discovery. If he has obtained rank and power, to keep them he is urged on to more murders, in order to silence accusation. Although he may be dead to any sentiment of humanity, yet his soul is tortured. Nothing affords him pleasure; he often wishes he had not bought, at the price of such suffering, what he thought would afford him satisfaction. Remorse assumes the expression of all the ugly passions of our soul—fear, terror, despair, anger, jealousy, such as are represented by the Figs. 16 to 34, Chap. XI., Physiognomy. This constant disorderly state of our soul impresses its marks on our countenance—the forehead becomes wrinkled, the eyes become sunken and assume a haggard and cruel expression, the lines at the sides of the nose and mouth become strongly marked. The action of the body is restless, the walk is uncertain, irregular. The hands are the very image of the soul, the fingers become nervous, feverish, restless. The unfortunate creature tormented by this terrible passion resorts in vain to dissipation. He cannot drown his conscience in wine, nor can he efface the memory of his deeds. He strikes his forehead with force or tears his hair in despair. Remorse may be caused by a revulsion of feeling in the soul towards nobler sentiments; in this case, it would assume the more gentle expression of repentance, such as that of Capulet, in the last scene of *"Romeo and Juliet"*:

> " As rich shall Romeo by his lady lie,
> Poor sacrifices of our enmity."

The expression of this passion would be that of grief or despair, Chapter XI. Although this feeling would cause the features to assume in time an expression of grief and suffering, yet the physiognomy will preserve a look of dignity, whilst the same sentiment being the result of terror caused by crime, would stamp the face with all the signs of disorderly passions. The expression of this former sentiment would take the form of repentance.

XV. SHAME.—The consciousness of a wrong action, and the fear of discovery cause this sentiment. In presence of our accuser, we endeavour to conceal our confusion by excuses which make us feel all the more ashamed as they are ill conceived and fail to impress those we most wish to persuade. Our restless attitudes, the nervous movements of our hands, the blush on our face, all tend to betray the disorderly state of our mind. If we are caught in the very act, we turn pale, our limbs tremble, we are struck dumb; unable to run away, our expression becomes that of dejection. We cast our eyes down, and cannot stand the accusing glance of others. As soon as we become fully aware of the ridiculousness in our position, or of the serious consequences attached to it, we cry, or resort to false assertions. If, for instance, our accuser points to an object we may have stolen, we instinctively hide it. If it be a moral wrong, for which we can find no excuse, we endeavour to give ourselves a countenance by seizing hold of some object, such as the skirt of our coat, or our hat, which we twist and turn in a nervous manner. Stubborn people keep still and silent, no earthly power can move them.

XVI. TIMIDITY.—This feeling is caused by an innate sentiment of fear. The apprehension of unknown danger seems to influence all the thoughts and actions of a timid and irresolute person. It is often the result of early education, when the mind may have been scared by dismal tales, dark cupboards and dark rooms. This sentiment is almost natural to woman, in whom sensibility and gentleness exist in greater proportions than in man. Timidity being the opposite of courage can only be expressed by mild gradations of fear, which is in itself the very reverse of the latter sentiment. A short walk, gentle and nervous actions, a subdued tone of voice are the signs of this feeling. Timidity often arises from an excess of prudence. We fear not being equal to our task ; we blush and tremble when we have to undergo examination.

XVII. SUSPICION.—Constant suspicion or anxious fear of being deceived, will cause a sort of diseased state of the soul more worthy of pity than anger for the unfortunate being who is troubled with it. This sentiment is often the result of experience. Youth is rarely suspicious, whilst old age is. There are two striking gradations in this sentiment—that of mistrust, and distrust or diffidence. There is a great difference between mistrust and distrust ; the first is the instinct of a timid and perverse nature ; the second is the result of experience and reflection. We are born with the first ; we acquire the second.

A mistrustful man judges of others by himself, and fears them.

A distrusting man reserves his judgment of others.

We mistrust the disposition and intentions of others ; we distrust or guard against their talent and wit. Distrust in oneself may be considered as a virtue if not carried to excess. It is said that too much confidence constitutes a fop, too much diffidence a fool. The suspicious man is one of the unhappiest beings in creation ; he does not believe in friendship, gratitude, or love, and suspects an interested motive in every sentiment. An inquiring and restless expression in the eye, shaking of the head, shrugging of shoulders, and a natural tendency to turn away from those who address us, are the general symptoms of this sentiment. The expression of the mistrusting man is anything but happy ; anxiety, care, suffering are pictured on his face. Like those of the miser or the hypocrite, his movements are nervous, cautious, never spontaneous ; his attitude and walk are timorous and undignified. On the contrary, modesty and reflection are the impressive signs of the diffident man.

# CHAPTER XVII.

---

## ON PRIMARY AND DERIVED SENTIMENTS.

IF we recapitulate the analysis contained in the preceding chapters, we find that some passions are rendered by expressions and actions peculiar to themselves, whilst others borrow their expressions from them, or from a combination of two or more sentiments. The first of these two classes of passions we shall call *primary*, the second *derived*.

Some sentiments are expressed by a simple action, others by a combination of contrary actions, Fig. 49, page 145. These sentiments we may call simple and compound.

We find in the analysis of Basilio's song in the "*Nozze de Figaro*," Chapter XXIV., sentiments that are expressed by metaphorical actions. These we should call figurative. Therefore, if we classify these different sentiments, we obtain the following table :—

Primary sentiments.
Derived sentiments.
Simple sentiments.
Compound sentiments.
Figurative sentiments.

All sentiments ought to be treated according to the above

order, giving at the same time the expression of the derived or secondary, the compound, and the figurative sentiments. The actions will be those of either of these classes, or of a modified combination of the two. *Pity* can only be rendered by the combined expression of love and suffering. *Kindness* is represented by the combined expression of love and veneration.—*Sorrow, despondency*, by the expression of suffering mixed with gentle veneration. *Mistrust* and *suspicion* betray themselves by the expression of secret grief, an anxious and furtive look, as well as a constant anxiety to listen to the conversation of others. *Clemency* is expressed by the appearance of love, modified by dignity or pride, *Hope* sees happiness or success in the future only; therefore it is never free from fear or doubt. It is accordingly expressed by a combination of eagerness and fear. *Malicious Joy* is rendered by the expression of hatred and contempt. *Envy* differs from suffering in expression and from hatred, inasmuch as the look is sly and often betrays shame. The eyes cannot stand the searching glance of others.

# CHAPTER XVIII.

GRADATION AND HARMONY TO BE OBSERVED
BETWEEN THE SENTIMENTS AND THEIR EX-
PRESSIONS.

IN connecting the different actions it is necessary to observe
certain gradations, according to the situation and movement
of a piece. For instance, an actor will not wait until he has
delivered the very last word of a sentence, to leave the stage
suddenly. On the contrary, he will gradually prepare his exit
during the latter part of his phrase, and quit the stage whilst
saying the last words; or, if the situation requires it, his very
last words will be followed by a pause, which will be all the more
impressive as the expression of his face and his action will continue
the effect of the sentence, and carry on the movement of the
piece without interruption until he has made his exit. In
comedy, when two people leave the stage together, they prepare
their exit whilst in conversation, and are almost out of sight
while still saying the last words. Precipitation between two
gestures, in fact want of repose in the general treatment of a
scene, completely destroys the illusion which the spectator would
otherwise feel. It is a common fault amongst young actors.
    Imagination never passes from one sentiment to another

without undergoing a certain gradation or intermediate and pro-gressive state; without these the transitions would be so vapid that the effect would be ludicrous, and for this very reason such abrupt transitions are admissible only in comic parts, or in scenes of madness, where the mind has lost all power of reasoning and passions follow each other without any sense or control. In Mdlle. Gay's (afterwards Madame de Girardin) Comedy in one Act, "*La joie fait peur*," we find such sentiments as are susceptible of the most exquisite and moving gradations in the human heart. In the 8th scene, when Adrien, the son of Madame des Aubiers, suddenly appears before Noel, the faithful old servant,—Régnier (the celebrated actor of the Comédie Française), who was performing the part,—at the sight of the unexpected young sailor whose reported death had broken the mother's heart, remained petrified; it was for him a dream, not a reality; gradually, as his doubts vanished, the reaction of joy took place;—he trembled, he tried to speak, but his voice faltered, the action of his heart stopped; he turned pale and fainted in young Adrien's arms. It would be useless to attempt to describe such acting. Régnier's emotion was so true, so natural, that scarcely any one present was able to repress his tears. The next scenes all work up to the last one, where Madame des Aubiers finds her son again. The admirable gradation intended by the author and so well observed by the actors—Régnier especially—made such an impression that it left in all the spectators an indelible memory.

Imagine, on the contrary, that some of the actors had suddenly awakened the mother's suspicions by an ill-timed joy or im-petuosity of manner, instead of careful and tender solicitude—the movement of the piece would have gone on with such force that nothing but the violent death of Madame des Aubiers could have formed a climax, and harmonised with the galloping rapidity of the sentiments.

If an actor, because he has a dramatic part to perform, comes on the stage looking fierce or overburdened by his passions before any actual scene has passed that justifies his fierceness of countenance; if, at the least provocation, he splutters, rants, roars, cries, and shows an uncalled-for exuberance of action, what will he do when the sentiment increases in intensity, or when a climax has to be reached? His only course will be to continue roaring and spluttering, until he gets hoarse and worn-out. The consequence will be, that, instead of working up to the paroxysm of passion by well-combined gradations, he will become weak when he ought to be full of energy and power. His voice will fail him; and in his anxiety to produce an effect, his acting will be outrageously overdone—he will be redundant in his gesticulation. This total disregard of gradation shows that actors neglect to observe Hamlet's advice :—

"Suit the action to the word, the word to the action; with special observance that you overstep not the modesty of nature," &c.

Such acting we should call *stagey*, or conventional and artificial; that is, when casting nature aside, the actor, instead of selecting action that would convey to the public a true expression of *real* sentiments, and using such a tone of voice as he would employ in ordinary or impassioned moments of life, adopts certain attitudes and gestures, and a certain way of mouthing, which he thinks specially suited to the stage, and which he certainly ought to discard. This error causes him, the very moment he steps upon the stage, to assume such a sad, gloomy, tragic expression, that before the first act is over, he has already exhausted the means of expressing such passions, as well-timed vigour, play of physiognomy, and power of voice would have enabled him to render with thrilling effect. Coleridge said that "seeing Kean act was like reading Shakespeare by flashes of lightning." To act by flashes of lightning is to observe such gradations as may allow of impulsive, sublime moments of passionate vigour. To draw a parallel, we may say that to act in the midst of constant storm is to fall short of the commonest understanding of human passions. The same may be said of such a part as that of Triboulet, in Hugo's "*Le Roi S'amuse.*" He is sarcastic but not boisterous; cruel and cutting with the noblemen of the court, he is servile and amusing with his master.

In passing from one sentiment to another the change may be more or less rapid, as there is more or less hesitation between the two sentiments to be exhibited. This depends on the state of our mind and the contrast existing between the sentiments. If we hear great news, whilst our mind is totally unprepared for it, we pass through a series of gradations until the sentiment of joy has replaced all other feelings. If, on the contrary, we partly expect the news, our soul being already full of expectation, we pass rapidly to the last stage of the highest contentment. For instance, when Tubal calls the attention of Shylock to the fact that, if he has lost his jewels other men have ill luck too, Shylock passes rapidly from the sentiment of grief and rage to that of joy. As Tubal contrasts his news of the extravagance of Shylock's daughter with the ruin of Antonio, the rapid change between two opposite sentiments is easily explained, if we bear in mind that Shylock comes on the stage already tortured by the loss of his property and incensed by the deceit of his daughter. Therefore the news of Antonio's misfortunes is received with avidity—a sentiment of joy rushes to the revengeful man's soul, and becomes all the more predominant as he anticipates the moment when his cruel vengeance will be satiated by taking the life of a hated Christian.

This sentiment of revenge so entirely engrosses his mind that all his thoughts and actions are consecrated on that one object. Supposing that Shylock had heard the news of his daughter's flight and of Antonio's reverses at the same time, it is evident that his passions would have undergone many gradations before the sentiment of despair had given way to that of malicious joy.

## HARMONY TO BE OBSERVED BETWEEN THE ACTION AND THE SENTIMENTS.

The first condition for an actor is to *look* the character he represents. His deportment and action, and the expression of his face, must be in perfect harmony with the sentiments he has to express. Garrick said to a French actor: " You performed your part of the drunkard admirably ; only, if I may be permitted to make an observation, your left foot looked awkward." No doubt Garrick meant to say that the actor's left foot did not look in harmony with the other parts of his body.

This evidently shows the importance of modifying or correcting the defects we may have naturally, or may have acquired by negligence. The toes turned in, the knees giving way, the head drooping on one side, would certainly not be in keeping with a sentiment of pride or dignity. The face must also be in harmony with the different sentiments or passions to be expressed. Young actors often fail in this; and although their youth and beauty may greatly favour them, yet the complete want of expression in the face shows that their mind is under the influence of fear or indecision, or that they do not feel the sentiments they have to express. As the features are not moved by any inward emotion, they remain impassible. The expression of the face is as cold as marble. All possible illusion is therefore lost for the spectator.

It is absolutely necessary that the actor should study thoroughly the general movement, not only of a piece as a whole, but of each separate scene, so as to harmonise his part with those of others; that is, he must know to regulate his acting according to the situation, and make it predominant or *subservient*, as the author intends it to be. If, in a dramatic scene, some actor of a subordinate part ventured on an ill-timed pantomimic action, although his part might be comic, he would either irritate the public, or cause laughter where a sentiment of sorrow or terror ought to animate the spectators; and, as Hamlet observed, "though it might make the thoughtless laugh, would cause the judicious to grieve." Again, if the principal actor were to monopolise the entire attention for himself, when the principal interest ought to bear on others, the effect of the scene would entirely miscarry. In dramas, the movement of the piece is often varied by the happy introduction of some cheerful or gentle sentiment, so as to give more effect to the tragic scenes, or in order to afford relief to the spectators. These are the lights and shades of the comedy or tragedy which prove highly effective if rendered with art and judgment.

However secondary may be the part he has to perform, let the actor remember that he forms part of a picture. The eyes of the public are upon him wherever he may be on the stage. Neglect, either in his deportment or actions, would mar the harmony of the picture.

Let the singer, as well as the actor, be careful never to forget himself after a monologue or a song. If the voice has ceased to be heard, the movement of the piece goes on just the same; therefore the action must continue, and the actor must carefully avoid throwing himself into such an attitude as to indicate that the moment has come for applause. The actor or singer who throws *true* feeling into his acting will always fairly win his reward. He must carefully avoid such intonations of voice or action as would express the contrary of what he means. For instance, to express a sentiment of terror with a composed action or a calm expression of the face, or to render every figurative sentiment by redundant gesticulation, would be simply absurd. When the king says to Hamlet:

"How is it that the clouds still hang on you?"

It would be laughable were he to point to the clouds, then to represent the act of hanging, and lastly to point to Hamlet. As this phrase is figurative, and amounts to a simple question, one single appropriate action, or even the searching eye of the King will express quite enough.

Riccoboni says, "People of the lower class, who easily give way to the impressions they receive, do not know how to control their feelings. They are the true models of strong expression. We see in them the dejection of grief, the crouching of the suppliant, the scornful pride of the conqueror, passion carried to excess, lastly, the great tragic feeling. Let us add to these a varnish of politeness, and it will be perfection. In one word, we must express ourselves like the people, and carry ourselves like noblemen."

# CHAPTER XIX.

---

### GESTURES, AND SUMMARY OF ACTION.

IN descriptive ballets the dancers have to express all their sentiments by pantomimic action. Mute actors, such as the dumb girl in "*Masaniello*," are also introduced. This sort of acting requires a great knowledge of the different gestures appropriate to each sentiment and passion. The first condition for a good pantomimist is to possess a face susceptible of great variety of expression—of great mobility. The very faults to avoid in tragedy or high comedy could be turned to good account in low comedy or comic parts. Symmetric, awkward movements prove very successful when judiciously used.—See Figs. 22, 23, 24, 25, pages 55 to 58.

Fig. 48, page 83, would correspond to the expression, "Do you see a mote in my eye?"—In mockery, the gestures are always exaggerated, as we endeavour to throw ridicule on others.

### SUMMARY OF DIFFERENT GESTURES.

A hat held in the hand, a three-cornered hat carried under the arm, the hand resting on a sword, give a graceful appearance when varied with other actions.

Taking or offering snuff was a very important act in the time of " Richelieu," when noblemen made a point of carrying a snuff box to imitate the Prime Minister.   Particular grace was displayed in delicately applying the tips of the fingers to the nose, and great care was taken not to soil the costly lace of the shirt or frill. Some carried richly inlaid *bonbonnières*, equal to a snuff box in size, but slightly different in shape.

Sneezing, coughing, winking, are resorted to as signs of warn-ing : also a touch with the elbow, which expresses doubt as well.

In eating and drinking, the actor must endeavour to represent the act of every-day life, and go through his meal with perfectly natural action, not letting the public see that he has only a " pro-perty" chicken on the table.   In one English play, by the way, it was long the stage tradition to introduce a real leg of mutton, sometimes to the great satisfaction of the hungry actors who took part in the scene.   It is always advisable to have some real eatable that the actor can put in his mouth.

In holding a glass or goblet, actors—and especially singers—whilst singing a drinking song, generally flourish it about, for-getting that it is supposed to be full of wine—or drain it with such rapidity that the illusion is really impossible.   Such errors must be carefully avoided.

In shaking hands, a lady will always present the hand nearest to the interlocutor.

In kneeling towards a person, the right knee will touch the ground if the actor is to the left of the public ; or the left knee if on the right side of the public.

Dresses with long trains require careful management on the part of ladies.   A quiet movement of the body in the act of turning, with a graceful and well timed touch of the hand, will keep the train in its place.   Kicking the dress back is not always a graceful movement.

Crossing each other on the stage must always be subservient to the requirements of the scene and have a motive.   It must be natural and never conventional.   We often see actors cross each other without any apparent reason, thinking, perhaps, that it breaks the monotony caused by standing in the same position.

In doing so, they are purely conventional. The crossing must be properly timed, and justified by the immediate action that follows.

In a paroxysm of terror or passion, the difficulty of breathing is often accompanied by a choking noise, caused by the contraction of the larynx. The reproduction of this action on the stage is of great effect when properly timed and judiciously resorted to.

Fencing is an art sadly neglected amongst actors and tragedians generally, who are constantly fighting on the stage. It requires skill and elegance, and ought therefore to be thoroughly studied under a master. An awkward thrust has often been the cause of an accident. In fighting a duel it is necessary to measure the ground, and settle beforehand on what part of the stage the fall or death will take place, so as to prevent confusion in the following scenes, which would destroy the harmony of the general picture.

A duel must be essentially conventional, unless it is represented by two actors perfectly masters of the art. The reason of this is that, instead of being a dignified and elegant action, it degenerates into a ridiculous struggle and confusion. Therefore to avoid this it is necessary that every thrust or guard should be studied, agreed upon, as well as numbered, so that every action should be well timed.

The action of bowing is based on the rules already explained, and is more or less respectful, as it is directed to an equal, a superior, or a lady. Grace and dignity form the essential part of its performance.

Salutation varies according to nationalities and degrees of intimacy.

The Turks raise the hands to the lips, and thence to their turban.

Italians and Spaniards raise their hats, shake hands or kiss each other, even in the streets. The French or English wave their hands or raise their hats. Amongst some of the actions we have seen in characteristic parts, we remember a French actor in

Paris playing the part of Fouinard in the "*Courrier de Lyons.*"
His attire being rather disreputable, he had a loose, worn old shoe
that kept dropping from his foot.   To keep it on he was compelled
to drag it on the ground; and if by any mischance he took a
hurried step the unfortunate shoe would drop off, which compelled
him to stop and get his foot in again, or, if running, to go back for
it.   This ridiculous mishap occurred when he was in the greatest
hurry or in the most tragic moment; the action was done with so
much nature and ease that it was quite a relief to the existing
scenes, and showed as a contrast of quaintness against the rascality
of his companion Choppard.

# CHAPTER XX.

---

### FAULTS TO BE AVOIDED ON THE STAGE.

ONE of the commonest errors amongst actors is, whilst addressing their interlocutors on the stage, to turn towards them, thus offering their side-face to the public. The persistent keeping of the head in this position has two great disadvantages. In the first place, the words being directed to the right or left are not distinctly heard by the public on the opposite side. In the second place, the expression of the face is only half seen by the spectators. In order to obviate this, it is necessary to observe the following rules :—

> *Firstly.* Avoid standing side by side with the person you are addressing.
>
> *Secondly.* Keep the body in the second position and three parts turned towards the public.

As the floor of the stage is composed of boards, it is an easy matter for the actors to keep the width of one or two boards between them ; for example :

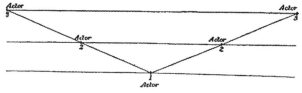

Either of the positions 1 and 2, or 2 and 3. This position is extremely favourable, especially when the scene is impressive and takes place between two actors. The speaker being on the second board, and in the second position, faces the public almost entirely, his words are clearly heard, the play of his physiognomy is distinctly seen. If actor No. 2 or No. 3 has an "aside" to say, he merely turns his head to the opposite side from his interlocutors, and has no need to move his body. The by-play of the listener, whose part may be to hide his emotions from his companion, is entirely exposed to the eye of the audience, who eagerly watch the different expressions of his face. This quiet although impressive attitude of the two actors adds greatly to the effect and power of a scene, which would fall flat were they to interrupt the movement and flow of the passions by a constant change of position, turning of heads and awkwardness of attitudes. If the dialogue between the two characters is rapid and animated an occasional and well-timed change of position may take place. The general rule to follow is this :—Let the actor fall back to the second board whenever he wishes to make an impression on others, and let him come forward to the first board whenever he has to receive an impression.

As the public is the first consideration for an actor, it is barely admissible that he should turn his back to the auditorium ; yet some exceptions are not only perfectly allowable, but may be the natural consequence of the requirements of some of the scenes. If we suppose several people, some sitting, others standing, round a fire place, the actor on whom devolves the principal interest of the scene, will, as a matter of course, assume the most prominent position, so that he may be seen and heard distinctly by the public, whom he would naturally face. The other characters being in the position of listeners, might consistently turn towards him, and thus stand with their backs to the spectators.

Thus, when the ghost of Hamlet's father appears at the side of the stage, he concentrates on himself, for a few moments, a great part of the public's attention ; it would not therefore be inconsistent for Hamlet to face the spectre, although he would by doing so partly hide his face from the audience. Should he persist in that position, Hamlet would have to raise the pitch of his voice slightly, and pronounce his words slowly, so that not a syllable should be lost.

When Othello is wound up to a state of wild passion by Iago's insinuations, he becomes so violent and abrupt in all his move-ments, that should he in his impetuosity be so regardless of theatrical conventionalities as to address him whilst his back was turned to the public, it would not only look perfectly natural, but even prove highly effective (Fig. 52, page 181). We may say that there is nothing awkward or ridiculous on the stage that is natural and well timed. Experience, taste, and a true love of the art are the safest guides for an actor.

## ON THE WANT OF HARMONY IN THE GENERAL ACTION AND THE SCENES.

One of the principal evils of the stage is, no doubt, the starring system, which is a source of endless abuses. Not only are the actors or singers, excepting *the star*, often totally unfit for their parts, but the scenery is utterly disregarded, so that, to hear one good performer, the public is compelled to undergo a succes-sion of painful sensations, which counterbalance, if they do not destroy, the pleasure given by the talent of the principal actor. Everything is sacrificed to that object, and the works of the great masters are entirely misrepresented. The actors are scarcely ever perfect in their "words," and the want of sufficient preparation in rehearsal is always perceptible. To single out some of the errors, we will mention facts we have witnessed in the performance of Shakespeare's tragedies, "*Othello*" and "*King Lear*." The first scene in the first act of "*King Lear*" is a state room in the King's palace. To say nothing of the slovenliness of the scenery in general, we will simply state that in the middle of the stage there is a plat-form, on which is placed an armchair, similar to a throne, and on each side two smaller armchairs. The King enters, followed by his three daughters and others; he takes his place on the throne;

FIG. 52.

Goneril sits at his right, Regan at his left hand, and, to complete the picture, Cordelia sits at the foot of the throne. As soon as Lear says "Goneril, our eldest born, speak first;" she gets up, takes three or four steps towards the footlights, and, turning her back to the public to address her father, she answers,—"Sir, I love you . . . " &c.; having ended her speech, she resumes her seat, close to her father. Then says the King: "Our dearest Regan, wife to Cornwall, speak!" Regan immediately gets up, walks up to the footlights, turns her back to the public, delivers her answer and goes again to her seat. Lastly, Cordelia answers her father in exactly the same attitude, her action being the fac-simile of that of her sisters. The consequence of such acting is this: in the first place, it is monotonous and unnatural to see three actresses do exactly the same thing, especially when one of them expresses sentiments totally different from those of the others. In the second place, the expression of their physiognomy is entirely lost to the public; and, thirdly, they are compelled to *rant* and shout their words in order to be heard. Thus, instead of the subtle music with which the voice ought to deliver the kind words of filial love, as intended by Shakespeare, we hear an unmusical and strained sound. Hamlet's advice to the actors would be quite applicable in this instance: "Speak the speech, I pray you, as I pronounced it to you, trippingly on the tongue; but if you mouth it, as many of your players do, I had lief the town crier spoke my lines."

To avoid these errors it would be far better for the three daughters to keep their places, and, by their graceful and varied attitudes whilst addressing their father, add a great charm to the gentle delivery of their loving words, without having to turn their backs to the public. It is true that by this latter attitude they act up to the King, who during the whole time holds the entire attention of the public, the other actors becoming mere figures in a background. If so what becomes of the harmony of the piece? Is it one person the public has come to see and hear, or a great tragedy worth attention in its minutest details? Shakespeare's words are thrilling whether in a king's mouth or in that of a knave; therefore to sacrifice any part of his great works is to disregard the intentions of a great writer.

Actors are apt to forget that the eyes of the spectators are fixed on them, and that none of their actions or looks escape criticism. Hence numerous mistakes are made, which ought to be carefully avoided. We have seen in the fifth act of "*Othello*," Iago standing behind the body of Roderigo, who is lying on the ground, wounded by Cassio; and whilst Roderigo says "Oh! murderous slave! oh! villain!" Iago *pretends* to drive his sword through his dupe's body (not stabbing him), leaning on the sword with great effort, changing at the same time the tone of his voice, as we are apt to do when we perform acts requiring great physical power. If the actor had turned his back to the public, and killed Roderigo quickly, we should not have seen where the sword went, but by the fact of his facing the public, every one could see it go into the floor, and this all the more distinctly as Iago made a great point of this most ludicrous action. In the same scene, when Cassio has wounded Roderigo, Iago, instead of wounding Cassio in the leg, thrusts him in the ribs. Whether such an unlucky thrust was the result of ignorance, or of too great a hurry, it matters not; the result was the same.

We will point out one more action, which we think is a decided error. In witnessing the same performance, we saw Othello, in the paroxysm of his passion, throw his cap in the air. This seems to us more the act of a boy, who for want of a stone throws his cap at another boy, and not at all in harmony with the temperament of a great warrior.

In the second act of "*Faust*" (Gounod), when Valentine, seeing that he has to deal with the Devil, holds up the cross-shaped hilt of his broken sword at Mephistopheles, the latter's nerves are so thoroughly overpowered by the sight, to him repulsive, that he helplessly shrinks from it. It grates upon his nerves as a sound out of tune grates upon the ear. The contraction of his features, the nervous twitching of his body, which he turns away from the hated symbol, are the expressive signs of his state of mind. Instead of this simple expression, it seems the accepted tradition amongst singers to crawl on all fours, as it were, from one side of the stage to the other, some biting their swords, others falling to the ground after having reached the opposite corner of the stage. This exuberance of action seems to us out of place, and if it has been adopted by one actor, it is no reason why every one should do the same. Moreover, what may be successfully done by one may be miserably bungled by another.

# CHAPTER XXI.

## MAKING UP THE FACE.

WE would recommend students of the dramatic art to study Chapter XI., on physiognomy, as it will assist them greatly in mastering the art of "making up" their faces; which art contributes in a great measure to the perfect harmony that must necessarily exist in the general appearance of an actor.

If we cannot materially alter the shape of our head, yet with the assistance of artificial means, such as wigs, beards, paint, &c., we can modify to a great extent the natural defects or our expression, so as to *look* the part we have to represent, although our natural face may differ from it.

A conscientious actor ought to make himself acquainted with the works of the painters, as he will acquire by their study the knowledge of general effects. The want of such knowledge causes an absence of accuracy in "making up" and dressing for a part, which betrays itself in the indiscriminate use of these artificial means. We may assert that if an actor is fully pene-trated with his part he will require but very few touches to complete a picture, which his action, words, and attitudes already greatly contribute to represent. Such lines as we see drawn in Lebrun's faces, Chapter XI., or as may be stamped by nature on our own or on others' faces, may serve as guides to trace, for instance, the wrinkles of old age. The first desideratum in making up is to look natural, taking into consideration the glare of the gas lights and the distance between the actor and the public. The strong light necessitates the use of artificial means in order to give an agreeable complexion, or to modify it, if dark or sanguine; otherwise the colour of the skin would look coarse and red. The make-up of the face must be regulated therefore according to the requirements of the complexion, and of the part to be represented. To obtain the desired results it would be advisable to experimentalise according to the following hints :—

Pearl white, rouge, and violet powder are the principal ingredients used to make up a young face, and are applied in the following manner: If the complexion is fair, simply spread some cold cream on the face, and with a puff put some violet powder or powdered magnesia. If the skin is dark, it is necessary to mix some pearl white with cold cream and spread it carefully, so as not to leave any patches. As this mineral white is crude in shade, it is desirable to soften it by passing violet powder over it, thus giving transparency to the complexion. The application of the rouge must begin immediately under the eyelashes and spread mostly on the bony part of the cheek, leaving the nose untouched. Want of discrimination in the use of rouge would cause the face to look like a highly-coloured doll; this would not harmonise with the natural complexion. The rouge and white must blend together. A thin line of dark brown traced over the lower eyelashes gives force of expression and brightness to the eyes.

For an African complexion, we should take amber brown, mixed with the smallest quantity of purple brown; this made into a very thin paste with cold cream or lard, would be a near approach to an African complexion. Care must be taken in all cases to spread over the colouring a dry powder of the same colour, mixed with a small quantity of magnesia or violet powder, so as to counteract the shiny appearance caused by the use of cold cream.

Ochre, mixed with a very small quantity of amber brown, would imitate a sallow complexion, such as we often see in old people.

Amber brown mixed with a smaller quantity of chrome, and the smallest possible quantity of purple brown, would imitate the dull colour of a Persian.

Wrinkles are traced or imitated by means of paste pencils, such as are to be had at theatrical hairdressers. Pure black is too crude and hard for this purpose, as it gives an unnatural appearance and makes up what we should call a "dirty" face. The colours must be as nearly as possible an approach to the natural colour of the skin. The actor must trace with the pencils the lines of the face, round the eyes, alongside the nose, and on the forehead, having previously spread a very thin coating of cold cream all over the face.

The eyebrows are whitened with pearl white (blanc de perle), mixed with cold cream. Violet powder or magnesia spread over the face, with or without any of the powders above mentioned, will blend all the colours together, and tone down the general make-up.

A bald wig requires a great deal of attention so as to look *natural*, as the colour given to it by the hairdresser rarely corresponds to that of our complexion. The line caused by the wig on the forehead is also very offensive to the eye. In order to avoid these contrasts it is necessary to spread a flesh-coloured pomatum on the wig and forehead, so as to blend the two together.

We recommend cold cream instead of water for the mixing of colours: not only does it spread evenly on the face without patches, but the perspiration does not affect it, nor does the skin get so easily injured.

Magnesia is an excellent substitute for violet powder—easy to get, cheaper, and free from chalk. A thin coating of amber brown mixed with a very small quantity of white and spread under the eyes gives them a sunken appearance.

Chrome and violet powder mixed together deaden the colour of the skin and gives a ghastly appearance. The same mixture can be made into a paste. When the eyes have a sunken appearance, rouge on the nose, and very little on the bony part of the cheek, with chrome mixed with white spread over the face, gives the appearance of a low, drunken type.

A thin coating of amber brown, spread in the hollow of the cheeks will make the face look thinner.

The combination of the eyes and cheeks being sunk, a thin coating of chrome mixed with white powder over the face will give the appearance of a dying person. In this case no rouge must be used.

A little crimson paste on the lips, as well as a little rouge on the tips of the ears, and also on the nails, will add freshness and transparency to the skin. Care must be taken to whiten the neck and hands.

There are many ways of making up the face that are more or less typical, and which words cannot possibly describe. It is for the actor to study the combination of colours and general effects, so as to *look* the part he has to play.

Many artistes carry this art to such perfection that they are scarcely recognisable on the stage.

It is said that the celebrated French actress Dejazet, who played the part of young lovers, at the age of 70, used to get rid of her numerous wrinkles by means of elastic wigs that kept the skin tightly drawn from the forehead.

Fig. 53.

Fig. 54.

In Figs. 53 and 54, we see the faces of two very old peopl
The lines may serve as a guide in tracing the wrinkles. Figs. 5
;6, 57, 58, 59, 60, 61, 62, 63, 64, may serve as guides in the u:
of wigs and moustaches.

FIG. 55.

FIG. 56.

FIG. 57.

N

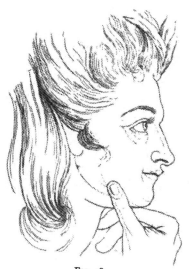

FIG. 58.

FIG. 59.

FIG. 60.

FIG. 61.

FIG. 62.

FIG. 63.

FIG. 64.

# CHAPTER XXII.

## ANALYSIS OF MARK ANTONY'S ORATION OVER THE CORPSE OF CÆSAR.

IN Act III., Scene II., of Shakespeare's "Julius Cæsar," Mark Antony, being requested by some of the Roman people to go up into the public chair, says:

"For Brutus' sake I am beholden to you!"

Upon their invitation he ascends the rostrum, his manner and looks betraying the sorrowful state of his mind. Facing the assembly, he waits until silence and order are restored; his looks and dignified attitude impressing all those around with the solemnity of the occasion. On his address depends the fate of his cause; he must win partisans to his side, and destroy the effect of the speech Brutus has just made, proving Cæsar to have been a tyrant. Although he professes not to be an orator, "as Brutus is," yet he delivers his speech with consummate ability; his eloquence is natural and spontaneous; he insinuates himself into the feelings of the people—tender and pathetic at first when he speaks of Cæsar, he becomes sarcastic when he speaks of his enemies. With consummate skill he uses such language as may be understood by all, and gradually changes the emphasis as he goes on, measuring his sarcasm by the feelings of his audience.

"Friends, Romans, countrymen, lend me your ears."

Having said these words with a solemn voice, he looks round
the assembly, and makes a pause until his words have produced
the desired effect.

" I come to bury Cæsar."

Here Mark Antony points, with a slow movement of the hand,
to the body lying on the hearse, and at some distance from him,
his eyes following the same direction; then raising them again,
full of grief, whilst the hand remains in the same position, he says
in a lower tone of voice :

" *Not* to praise him."

The hand having fallen down again as if powerless, he continues
in a higher pitch :

" The evil that men do lives after them ;<br>
The good is often buried with their bones : "

and whilst saying in a lower tone :

" So let it be with *Cæsar*,"

his hand will again point to the body, whilst the eyes will follow
the same direction.    After a short pause he gazes upon the
assembly, and dropping his hand, he exclaims :

" The noble Brutus<br>
Hath told you Cæsar was *ambitious*."

On this last word he raises his right hand suddenly, pointing
upwards with the first finger, thus adding force to this accusation.

" If it were so, it was a grievous fault."

During this phrase he lowers his hand to the level of his face
with a slight movement indicating acknowledgment, whilst the
left hand is extended forward, level with the waist, expressing the
same sentiment :—

"And grievously hath Cæsar answer'd it."

Here Antony looks down upon the body and shakes his head in
sorrow, whilst his hands drop down one after the other.    Raising
his head again, after a moment's pause, he proceeds—

" Here, under leave of Brutus and the rest—<br>
For Brutus is an honourable man ;<br>
So are they all, all honourable men."—

While delivering these lines he assumes the expression of sincerity, as if acknowledging an undoubted fact. The hands will be slightly spread forth, as if offering the fact for their consideration.

"Come I to speak of Cæsar's funeral."

Here the hands are slightly spread in a downward direction, with the palms upwards.

"He was my friend—faithful and just to me."

Here the head is gently shaken, the eyes being fixed on the body and the hands kept in the same position as in the last lines.

"But Brutus says he was ambitious;"

In saying this, the eyes are fixed on the body, the hands as before, the voice being solemn, low-pitched, and vibrating.

"And Brutus is an honourable man."

Here the actor will raise his head, his face assuming a slightly sarcastic expression, by a faint smile and a slight frowning of the eyebrows, the left hand making a *slow* movement up and down, the action this time being less decided in its assertion, the right hand having dropped down first.

"He has brought many captives home to Rome."

In saying these words, his face and voice brighten up, both hands advancing rapidly towards the body with the palms upwards.

"Whose *ransoms* did the *general coffers* fill."

Here the voice becomes clear and is pitched high, whilst the hands emphasise the fact by an abrupt and decided movement, with the palms upwards.

"Did this in Cæsar seem ambitious?"

This question is asked slowly, with a low and sonorous voice, whilst the arms are folded on the chest, the head being moved with a decided movement on the word *ambitious*, and raised as in the act of interrogating.

"When that the poor have cried,"

These words are said with a touching pathos, in rather a loud voice, whilst the arms are unfolded, and extended forward with a movement, offering the fact to the listeners; the following words are spoken in a lower and tearful voice—

> "Cæsar hath wept,"

the eyes of Antony being filled with tears.

> "Ambition should be made of sterner stuff."

This sentence is uttered with energy, and the face already betrays a sentiment of contempt, whilst the right hand is raised above the head with a sort of energetic flourish. Here a pause will be observed, so as to allow the words to make their impression. After a short moment, the left hand drops, the right arm slowly following the same movement.

> "*Yet* BRUTUS says HE was am*b*itious."

A scornful, low, and sonorous voice will utter this sentence.

> "And Brutus is an honourable man."

This is said rather slowly, with a slightly sneering voice and a somewhat sarcastic expression of the face, both hands being raised and moved with a similar expression without presenting the palm to the public, the head nodding in doubtful assent.

> "You all did see that on the Lupercal
> I thrice presented him a kingly crown,
> Which he did thrice refuse."

The voice here is pitched high; the right hand presents the fact to the auditors, being again raised higher and lowered immediately to the same level on the last words "thrice refuse." The left hand is advanced also slightly with the palm up, but without assuming so important an expression.

> "Was this ambition?"

Here the two hands are spread symmetrically forward, asking the question with great vehemence, the face being full of eagerness and energy, the eyes fixed in the distance.

> "Yet Brutus says he was ambitious."

This sentence is spoken with force, the hands remaining in the same position as in the last words—

"And, sure, he is an honourable man."

The left hand is raised as high as the head on the words "and sure," whilst the voice says them with a loud and abrupt tone, the face assuming an expression of sarcastic sincerity ; after a full stop the speaker continues with irony, "He is an honourable *man.*" Here the left hand is lowered level with the right hand, both offering the fact to the audience, whilst the pitch of voice is lowered and modulated into an insinuating tone, a sort of disparaging smile spreading over the face :

"I *speak not* to disprove what Brutus spoke."

On the words "*speak not*" the left hand is raised, the first finger being slightly shaken, the right assuming a secondary expression.

"But *here I am* to speak what I do know."

On the words "*here I am*" both hands are lowered, with an authoritative movement, the palm not quite turned up, the left retaining a higher position. The head will give strength to the words "what I do know" by one decided movement down and up.

"You all did *love* him *once,* not without cause."

The hands are spread apart, with the palms upwards, the voice being raised on the word "*love*," and doleful, as though in memory of the past, on the words "not without cause."

"What cause withholds you, then, to mourn for him?"

The hands are kept as above, the voice being raised higher, and in the interrogative.

"Oh ! judgment, thou art fled to brutish beasts,
And men have lost their reason."

These words are said more in despair than in bitterness. They are meant as a reproach rather than as a disparagement to their moral faculties. Antony's purpose was to persuade his hearers, and certainly *not* to offend them. In the first part of this sentence, the right hand drops down, whilst in the second part, "Men have lost their reason," the left hand is raised, and immediately after slowly dropped, as in despondency.

> "Bear with me "—(a pause)—
> " My heart is in the coffin there with Cæsar,"

pointing to the body with the flat of the right hand, the eyes full of tears and raised to heaven, as though in contemplation of his soul.

> "And I must pause till it come back to me."

Here the speaker will cover his face with his hands, sobbing silently. Antony's grief is dignified and impressive.

Having lowered his hands and looked round the assembly, he gives them time to comment on his words. Then, when silence has been restored, the speaker continues:

> " But yesterday the word of Cæsar might
> Have stood against the world."

This phrase is said with force whilst the hand is raised above the head, with the forefinger pointing upwards:

> " Now lies he there."

This is said after a pause, the left hand dropping, whilst the right hand presents its palm and extends towards the body at the same time:

> "And none so poor to do him reverence."

The speaker must avoid looking too often at the body: the eyes constantly lowered lose their expression, and that sameness of action would be monotonous and unimpressive.

> " Oh, masters, if I were disposed to stir
> Your hearts and minds to *mutiny* and *rage*."

This phrase, begun softly, becomes louder, more vigorous, and lastly very forcible both in tone and actions, when it comes to the words *mutiny* and *rage ;* this first insinuation being thrown out, Antony goes back quickly to his first tactics, and with a sort of reticence, he adds—

> " I should do Brutus wrong, and Cassius wrong,
> *Who*, you *all know*, are honourable men."

A soft insinuating inflexion of voice with a strong emphasis on the words "*all* know," and the same movements as in the preceding similar phrase will express this sentence :—

> " I will *not* do them wrong : I rather choose
> To wrong the dead, to wrong myself, and you,
> Than I will wrong such *honourable* men."

This is said with a loud voice, almost pompously, with warm action, as though Antony wanted to work himself into the persuasion of his own words : on the word " honourable "—which is pronounced with emphasis—an involuntary expression of contempt will suffice to deny the assertions he has just made. The right hand in this sentence will assume the principal action, and will rise with a slight undulation of the wrist level with the head, and as though throwing the honourableness of "*such honourable men*" to the winds.

> " But here's a parchment with the seal of Cæsar—
> I found it in his closet : " '*tis his will !*"

The last words are pronounced with great solemnity, whilst the eyes that were lowered on the parchment are raised to the audience in saying, "'*tis his will.*"

> " Let but the commons hear this testament
> (Which, pardon me, I do not mean to read) "

The latter part of this sentence is uttered as a remonstrance, whilst what follows will be declaimed with all the warmth, tenderness, and richness of tone of which a musical voice is capable.

> "And they would go and kiss dead Cæsar's wounds,
> And dip their napkins in his sacred blood ;
> Yea, beg a *hair of him* for memory,
> And, dying, mention it within their wills,
> Bequeathing it, as a rich legacy,
> Unto their issue."

On the words "And kiss dead Cæsar's wounds," the right hand, lying flat, will tremble as it points to the body. The left hand will do the same (the right keeping the same position) ; on the words "dip their napkins," &c., &c., both hands will drop at the end of the phrase.

> "Have patience, gentle friends; I *must not* read it."

In this sentence the hands are extended forward with the palms downwards, and on the words "I *must not* read it" the speaker will make a gentle authoritative movement with the first finger of the right hand, whilst the voice assumes a tone more in supplication than command.

> "It is not meet, you know how Cæsar loved you."

Here the hands are kept in the same position as in the above sentence.

> "You are not *wood*, you are not *stones*, but *men*."

On the word "*wood*" the left hand extends forward with the palm up, on the word "*stones*" the right hand follows the same action, and on the word "*men*" the speaker will strike his chest with the right hand, and with force. The voice, at first impressive and rather subdued on the first two words, will become solemn on marking an emphasis on "*men*," the face changing from contempt to sublimity. After a pause, he continues:

> "And being men, hearing the will of Cæsar,
> It will inflame you."—

The voice gradually acquires force, whilst the hands tremble with emotion.

> "It will make you mad!"

Here the climax is reached. Voice and actions express violent sentiments; the left hand will press the forehead with force and lower itself violently, as though Antony wanted to throw his own passion into the very soul of his audience. The right hand may retain the same position as in the preceding words.

> "'Tis good you *know not* that *you are* his *heirs*."

This is said with a sort of pacifying voice, whilst the right hand and first finger point to the public on the word "*you*."

> "For if you *should*, oh, what would come of it!"

The word "should" is uttered with force, and the left hand is suddenly raised high, with the palm facing the audience, whilst the end of the sentence is said with a subdued threatening tone— the face assuming a fatal expression, and the eyes shutting as though avoiding the sight of the terrible consequences.

Antony, who uses all the artifices and resources of a consummate orator, makes a long pause in order to excite the eager curiosity of the people to see the will, and also pretends to resist their request to show it until they have worked themselves into frantic excitement. Then, with authoritative tone, gestures, and looks, he says:

> "Will you be patient? will you stay awhile?"

He then proceeds, with a feigned penitent tone :

> "I have o'ershot myself to tell you of it !
> I fear I wrong the *honourable* men
> Whose daggers have stabbed Cæsar ; I do fear it !"

The first line is said with affected pathos, the hands pointing in the direction they have taken in leaving the stage.

"Whose daggers" (one hand drops) "have stabbed Cæsar," (the other points to the body, the face looking down upon it with intense sorrow, whilst the voice becomes solemn and impressive). "I do fear it" is said slowly, with an expression of revengeful sarcasm.

Having thus led the people to an almost complete revulsion of sentiments, Antony feels the time has come to appeal more directly to their tender feelings, which he skilfully does before showing the will which he knows must be the culminating argument against Cæsar's murderers.

> "You will compel me, then, to read the will?"

This question is asked as if Antony yielded only to the pressure put upon him by the people.

> "Then make a ring about the corpse of Cæsar,
> And let me *show* you *him* that *made* the will."

o

On the word "*him*" the hands are extended towards the body, the voice being raised with great pathos.

> "Shall I descend ? and will you give me leave ?"

At the bidding of the people Antony descends among them ; and being closely surrounded by the mob, whilst he directs his steps towards the hearse he exclaims with imploring accents :

> "Nay, press not so upon me ; stand far off."

Having come up to the body he prepares his effect by a skilful gradation, first recalling to the memory of the people the victory over the Nervii, pointing out to them the very mantle Cæsar wore for the first time on that day ; then showing them the rents made by the murderers' daggers, and the blood that covers it ; and, lastly, he uncovers the body, which they are now ready to mourn and weep over :

> "If you have tears, prepare to shed them now—
> You all do know this mantle."

Antony points to it with both hands, looking all round the assembly in order to render his words more impressive and to engross their full attention :

> "I remember
> The first time ever Cæsar put it on."

This is said with sorrowful expression, both hands dropping to the sides, the face looking at Cæsar, the head nodding in grief :

> "'Twas on a summer's evening, in his tent,
> That day he overcame the Nervii."

Then Antony raises his head with pride—his voice becomes animated :

> "*Look !* in *this place* ran Cassius' dagger through ;
> See what a *rent* the *envious* Casca made !"

He points to the different places with suppressed anger—his looks are terrible, his voice is the cry of passion :

> "Through this the well-beloved Brutus stabb'd ;
> And, as he pluck'd the *cursed* steel away,
> *Mark* how the blood of Cæsar follow'd it,
> As rushing out of doors, to be resolv'd
> If *Brutus* so unkindly knock'd, or no."

This sentence is delivered with passionate rapidity, the voice increasing in power and reaching its climax on the word "resolved," modulating again towards a tone of doubt on the last line. On the word "*mark*" both hands point trembling to the wound, whilst Antony turns to the people with a look of terrible anger :

> " For Brutus, as *you know*, was Cæsar's angel."

This is said with a desponding accent and expression, suggestive at the same time of Cæsar's greatness of heart and Brutus's ingratitude.

> "Judge, oh, you gods, how *dearly* Cæsar *lov'd* him."

Here Antony might kneel by Cæsar's body, appealing to the gods both with arms and face.

> " This was the most unkindest cut of all ;
> For when the noble Cæsar saw him stab,
> Ingratitude, more strong than traitor's arms,
> Quite vanquished him—then burst his mighty heart ;
> And in his mantle muffling up his face,
> Even at the base of Pompey's statue,
> Which all the while ran blood, great Cæsar fell."

During this sentence Antony's voice struggles with emotion. Tears flow from his eyes, his hands touch the wounds with tenderness, he leans over his beloved friend, and on the last few words he looks up to heaven, showing to his hearers the agony of his soul :

> " Oh ! what a fall was there, my countrymen ;
> Then I, and you, and all of us fell down,
> Whilst bloody treason flourished over us."

These words are uttered with great persuasion, the grieved soul of Antony giving way to intense sorrow, as though the destiny of a great nation had been crushed by the death of its ruler.

> " Oh, now you weep, and I perceive you feel
> The dint of pity."

Antony gets up again, his arms extended towards his overcome people :

> " These are gracious drops,
> Kind souls, what ! weep you, when you but behold
> Our Cæsar's *vesture* wounded ? "

Antony turns from one to the other, addressing them tenderly
with tears in his own eyes, extending his palms to them as in
gratitude :

> " Look you here,
> Here is *himself*, marr'd, as you see, with traitors."

In saying this Antony removes the mantle from the body, and,
dropping it at the foot of the corpse, hides his face in his hands,
sobbing at the infinite mournfulness of the sight.

> " Stay, countrymen ! "

Here Antony uncovers his face, and spreading his arms right and
left as in warm supplication, he utters the following sentence :

> " Good friends, sweet friends, let me not stir you up
> To such a sudden flood of mutiny ;
> *They* that have done *this deed* are *honourable*."

This last line is said with a suppressed tone of voice, the action
of the left hand and the angry looks pointing to the body, the
right hand having dropped ; whilst on the word "*honourable*" a
forced smile full of a terrible sneer overspreads the face, both
hands spreading in assent, the movement of the head expressing
the same idea.

> " What private griefs they have, alas ! I know not,
> That made them do it,—they are wise and honourable."

On the words "alas ! I know not" the right hand moves as if in
the act of rejecting, whilst the left arm drops of its own weight ;
and on the words "that made them do it" the right arm drops
heavily, the head turning towards the body, shaking slowly, and
the face and voice assume a solemn expression.

After a long pause Antony says, as if waking from a terrible
dream, and with a slow and unbelieving tone :

> " They are wise," &c.

Raising his voice suddenly, and with an intonation that challenges
the truth of his very words, he exclaims :

> " And will, no doubt, with reasons answer you."

The following lines are declaimed with modest, persuasive accents. As a contrast to the latter part of his "oration" Antony pretends to reverence Brutus and others and humbles himself before them, but gradually insinuates fury and revenge into the hearts of his listeners; and the more he seems to laud their "honour" and "wisdom," the more he exposes their villany and cowardice. The actions suitable to the next ten lines are those of offering the facts to the people, pointing to the body on the words "to speak of him," but on the words "to stir men's blood" the right hand, with the fist closed, strikes the heart with force, whilst the teeth are clenched, the face is fierce, and the voice trembles with concentrated passion :

> "Show you sweet Cæsar's wounds, poor, poor dumb mouths,
> And bid them speak for me."

This is said with tears in the eyes and voice, the left hand first pointing to the corpse, and afterwards both hands clasping each other, as we do in the paroxysm of our passions. The next sentence,

> "But were I Brutus," &c., &c.,

is declaimed with sudden force and passion, the eyes full of fire and revenge, the actions vigorous and telling. The right arm strikes the chest on the words "*there* were an Antony," the left hand is extended trembling towards the body on the words "and put a tongue in every wound of Cæsar;" whilst on the words "that should move the stones," &c., &c., the hands meet above the head and are suddenly spread on each side, whilst the face assumes such an expression as would, indeed, turn men's hearts into a furnace of devouring fire.

Fig. 56.

# CHAPTER XXIII.

---

## ANALYSIS OF THE ACTIONS IN SINGING.

### THE JEWELS SONG, FROM GOUNOD'S "FAUST."

THE difficulty in combining singing and acting is to harmonise the action with the words and the music. The constant repetition of the same sentiments and phrases, found in passages, concerted pieces, &c., the long notes extending over several beats or bars, often puzzle the singer to know what to do in order to be calm without being cold, and effective without any exuberance of action. Too great a demonstrativeness in acting spoils the effect of the voice and music, as the attention of the public is drawn in another direction.

In the buffo or brilliant style, such as the part of Geronimo in "Matrimonio Segreto," or of Figaro in "The Barber of Seville," the singer must be a thorough actor, as he has to depend as much on rapid and clear enunciation of words and on perfect acting as on the beauty of the voice—in fact, the latter enters as a secondary consideration, especially in the buffo style, where merriment and laughter are being constantly provoked by the facetious remarks and comical gestures of the actor. On the contrary, in all other styles the action must be to the music and the voice as a frame is to a picture; it must ornament, but not overpower it. In analysing the Jewels Song in Gounod's "Faust" I shall endeavour to describe, as far as words permit, the action and attitudes suitable to the different sentiments.

As Marguerite appears on the stage her walk is slow, her eyes are cast down, her arms hang listless at her sides, her general appearance being that of sadness. After advancing towards the public she lifts up her eyes, and pauses to say:

"I wish I could but know who was he that addressed me—if he is noble, or, at least, what his name is."

Whilst saying the last four words she walks slowly to the left, and sits down close to her spinning-wheel.

During the first five bars of the A minor melody, she works the treadle of her wheel with her foot, whilst her hands are occupied in twisting the flaxen thread and her head and figure gracefully bend over the work. The same attitude and action continue whilst she sings:

"O'er the sea in Thule of old, reigned a king who was true-hearted."

Suddenly she stops working, and looking up with an expression of sadness, says:

"He was so gentle in his bearing : his voice was so kind"—

referring, of course, to Faust. Having dismissed this thought, she resumes her singing and working. After the next twenty bars the same thought crosses her imagination; again she stops treading her wheel, and says:

"I knew not what to answer, and blushed like any child."

In the next thirteen bars which end the ditty she continues with the same occupation, singing whilst she twists her thread. As soon as she has done working, her imagination wanders back to the thought of Faust, and she says:

"'Tis but a lord who has so brave a mien ; so tender all the while."

During this phrase she gets up, and, whilst slowly advancing to the middle of the stage, in the direction of her cottage, she exclaims:

"No more ; 'tis idle dreaming."

She stays her course, and then, advancing towards the public, sings:

"Dear Valentine, may Heaven bless thee ! and bring thee home again."

During these words her eyes are raised to heaven, the two hands following the same direction ; and as she says "I am left here so lonely" the hands gradually fall back to their former position, the eyes are lowered, and the walk towards the cottage is sadly resumed.  As she nears the door she is agreeably surprised to see a bunch of flowers left on the steps by Siebel, her youthful admirer.

"Ah ! flowers laid there, no doubt, by Siebel."

She takes up the flowers, and, advancing again towards the public, says:

"Poor faithful boy !"

She sees in them a mark of attention, a token of affection, which causes in her a gentle sentiment of gratitude.  Whilst playfully handling her flowers she turns back towards her cottage, and as she is on the point of resuming her quiet walk, her eyes suddenly catch sight of the rich casket put by Mephistopheles close to where the flowers were.  She then exclaims:

"What is this?"

Here we have a kind of surprise very different from the first. Marguerite's feelings at the sight of the flowers are agreeable, but not novel.  Probably Siebel has surprised her in the same way many a time before.  But the sight of the casket is altogether unexpected.  Her astonishment is almost rapturous, her eagerness to seize the object is intense, and yet she has doubts and fears. Here the singer will do well to pause for a moment and observe the gradations that take place between these different senti-ments, namely :—

    I. Astonishment    -      -    At the sight of the casket.
   II. Eagerness -        -      -    Desire to take it.
  III. Doubt        -      -      -    Shall she take it?

The action suitable to each of these sentiments would be thus :

"What do I see there?"

She stops suddenly, and drops the bunch of flowers. She takes a few quick steps in the direction of the casket, and, after turning towards the public, extends her left hand towards the coveted object ; but she withdraws her hand immediately, saying :

"And by whom can the casket have been left?"

which she says to the public, the right hand meantime extending towards the spectators, as though emphasising the question. The attraction is great. She looks eagerly at the beautiful casket, and yet she is afraid of it ; for she says :

"I dare not touch it ; though the key is laid beside it, will it open?"

Finally her eagerness to see the contents overrules her fear, and after saying

"Why not? I may open, at least, since to look will harm no one."

Marguerite deliberately seizes the casket and the stool or garden chair on which it is placed, and carries it in front of the stage, kneeling down before it as she begins to bring the jewels out. Let the artiste give herself full time in order to develop with due effect the gradations that take place between the first moment of surprise and the instant she seizes hold of the casket.

As soon as she has opened the box, she clasps her hands with innocent joy and exclaims :

"Oh, heaven ! what gems with magic glare deceive my eyes."

On saying this she turns to the public (remaining all the while in her kneeling position), and expresses by her face the rapture of her soul ; and, whilst retaining the same position, she sings :

"Oh, never in my life did I dream of aught so lovely !"

During the next three bars she anxiously looks round, to see if she is not watched, and, taking the different jewels in her hands, says :

"If I dared but for a moment to try these earrings so splendid."

Here Marguerite shows by the eagerness of her actions and features her increasing desire, and yet her countenance is not quite free from a lingering sentiment of fear.  Having said this last phrase to the public she turns again towards the casket, and, seeing at the bottom of it a looking-glass, she sings :

"Ah! and here by chance, at the bottom of the casket, is a glass."

In saying this she ceases touching the jewellery, and expresses her joyous astonishment by stretching her hands towards the glass ; and again clasping them on her bosom (the action of both hands being symmetrical), she says to the public :

"Who could resist it longer?  Who could resist it longer?"

the repetition of this last phrase being accompanied by the turning of the *head* only towards the casket, the hands remaining in the same position.  During the next seven bars she takes the jewels out of the box, and, exposing them before the public, admires them one after another.  This by-play will continue for the next ten or twelve bars, when Marguerite will put on the earrings ; and whilst looking at herself in the glass, with the pleasure, grace and innocence of a young girl, she says :

"Is it I?  Come, reply!  Mirror, mirror, tell me truly!  No, no! 'tis not I!  No; surely enchantment is o'er me !"

In saying this she shakes her head, as if doubting her own identity.

"High-born maiden I must be, high-born maiden I must be.  This is not I, this is not I ; but a noble and king shall pay homage before me."

Here Marguerite gets up, and more as an *imitation* of what she *fancies* than the expression of what she really feels, she walks to and fro, assuming a mock dignity, which is extremely pleasing and graceful.

"Ah! might it only be, he could my beauty see, now as a royal lady, he would, indeed, adore me."

During this phrase, which extends over seventeen bars, Marguerite's feelings are mixed with a tinge of sentimental humour, which contrasts with the exuberance of her joy—her heart speaks as she alludes to Faust, who, she thinks, would love her if he saw her thus adorned. The actress must not fall into a very common error, which is to declaim the words,

"As a royal lady he would, indeed adore me,"

with great declamatory force. She must not forget for a single instant that Marguerite is an innocent loving girl, not a Medea or a Lady Macbeth.

During the next ten bars played by the orchestra, she resumes her position before the casket, and says :

"There are more ready to adorn me, None is here to spy—"

(She throws a furtive glance round)

"The necklace, the bracelet white, a string of pearls."

(These she puts on with marked delight.)

The remainder of the song, being a repetition of the same sentiments, must be treated throughout in the way that we have hitherto described, avoiding, in the last bar, especially, any aiming at effect, by attitudes and action incompatible with the simple and graceful manner of Marguerite.

# CHAPTER XXIV.

## ANALYSIS OF BASILIO'S SONG IN THE "NOZZE DI FIGARO."

THE analysis of this scene shows us that prudence is its fundamental moral. It is engrossed by figurative sentiments and metaphorical actions. In the recitation or dialogue that precedes the song, the following conversation takes place :—

> BARTOLO—" What's all this business ? "
> BASILIO—" Nothing ; Suzanna's caught his lordship's fancy, so she has granted him a meeting, which Figaro objects to."
> BARTOLO—" Of course ; would you then have taken it kindly ? "
> BASILIO—" What so many must suffer, why should he be exempt from it ? If he take umbrage, what great gain will be his ? As wags the world, friend, he who jostles the great ones, will have cause soon to blubber ; twenty points in his favour won't win him the rubber."

In this dialogue Bartolo's manners are in accordance with his impetuous nature, short and decided, and his voice loud. Basilio, on the contrary, is unctuous, hypocritical and insinuating. His walk is gliding, his voice subdued, his movements cautious and mysterious. He often looks round to see if he is watched. Being well penetrated with this sentiment of suspicion, the singer will be able to render this song with appropriate action, such as one might fancy in such a man. The gestures must be few, moderate in character, and expressive. This result can be obtained by keeping the elbows pretty close to the body; the hands moving above the waist, and kept rather close to the chest. In this position an infinite variety of action can be obtained, without being too demonstrative—but quite expressive enough, especially if the face is brought into active play. The sentiment throughout the song, bearing on a humorous sense of *warning*, and devoid of any passion ; the movements need no gradations, therefore can be symmetrical; the figurative way in which Basilio illustrates the advantage of being humble before superior power is ludicrous, and can only be rendered by ludicrous action. In the fifteenth bar, when he says:

> " Finding honour of profit sterile,
> From my head she chased the whim."

The action appropriate to this phrase would be to shake the first finger, as being the corroborative movement of an accomplished fact.

> " Near a cottage, poor and prim,
> She my footsteps led one morning."

Here the eyes and the first finger of the hand will follow the direction of the cottage, the body leaning slightly forward towards the same point.

> " Something she caused to tumble, those
> Neglected walls adorning :
> 'Twas a donkey's hide when near it."—

The first part of this phrase will be accompanied by a mysterious look and a gesture of indecision ; whilst the second part, which dispels all doubt, will be accompanied by an expression of joyful astonishment ; the hands and arms opening symmetrically and at a good distance from the body.

> " Take it, son—said she, and wear it ;
> Then she fled away and left me there."

Here a quick movement will indicate the act of giving something away.

> " Mutely as I on her stood gazing."

In saying this, the singer might fold his arms on his chest, and whilst singing the following phrase,

> "Sudden the thunder roar'd,
> Lightning's flash blazing ; hail,
> Rain in torrents pour'd,
> 'Twixt helter, skelter, though 'twas a pelter,"

he will divert his looks towards the skies. His arms unfolding rapidly, and his hands extending upwards, will add great force to this description of the storm.

> " I found a shelter under
> This ass's hide she bade me wear."

The action descriptive of this sentiment would be for Basilio to cover his chest and shoulders with his arms and hands, shrinking himself, as it were, under his skin to protect himself from the rain.

> "When storm and rain allay, two steps advancing,
> Some wild beast in my way stood fiercely glancing,
> To munch me, swallow, and crunch me ;
> Nothing lay before me save dark despair."

To illustrate these words the face must express fear, whilst one of the hands points to the place where the beast is supposed to be, the body assuming a sort of crouching position.

> "When from my skin the smell foully exhaling,
> O'er the beast's appetite even prevailing,—
> Sickened, and turned him back to his lair."

Basilio, in his descriptive fear, will cross both hands flat on his chest as though to protect it, and will preserve a motionless attitude until the beast is supposed to have retired.

> "From this adventure I gained this instruction,
> Tempests and outrages, e'en threatened destruction,
> Hurt not, an ass's skin if you but wear."

An authoritative movement of the hand will suffice to give strength to this assertion.

# APPENDIX.

# THE STAGE, AND
# ACTING IN ANCIENT TIMES.

―――

## GREECE.

IT is not without interest to study the different phases through which the stage and its organisation have passed, as well as the remarkable changes which have taken place in the social position of its votaries, in the different periods of history. Since the first germs of civilisation have sprung from the East, we must go back as far as the Greeks to reach the source whence the various arts, music, sculpture, tragedy, and comedy, diffused themselves over the world, spreading the taste and love of the beautiful, with imperishable effects. To the Greeks we owe the first idea of festivities systematically arranged in the form of public performances, as well as the construction of theatres. The celebration, of these festivities, was attended with very large expenditure, since they took place in immense theatres, capable, we are told, of holding thirty thousand spectators; large sums of money being also expended upon competitions, comprising music, the plastic arts, poetry, with choruses and dithyrambic and rhapsodic recitations. These emulative gatherings or solemnities, in which all the citizens participated, were held in honour of the gods; therefore, being religious institutions, they gave a taste

for art and poetry, and helped to spread those noble sentiments
which afterwards developed in the Grecian tragedies.  It was not
until these solemnities had lost their primary religious character,
that abuses led to the ruin of the state.   Instead of offering
sacrifice to the gods, the people began to squander their means in
luxury, and indulged in endless festivities.   Instead of employing
their resources in carrying on their wars and strengthening their
fleet, they lavished their wealth on bacchanalian revelry and
pomp.

The historical origin of the drama, especially in a country
endowed with a sunny and genial climate, where the imagination
of the people must have been very vivid, cannot be assigned to a
definite period.   We can only trace it from the age of history,
and assign its cause to the natural tendency of the people, especially in those countries, to combine poetry with worship.   This
sentiment led them to represent the deities in the shape of their
own work.   Hence may be deduced the origin of all arts,—painting,
sculpture, architecture, and music,—enlisted in the service of
prayer.   The love of personification being thus inspired, the
inhabitants of Southern Europe, especially, soon began to give
the human form to the objects of their adoration, and afterwards
gave to each a dwelling-place,—hence sculpture and architecture ;
they sang the praises of their gods,—hence poetry and music.

As regards their dances we may attribute these ceremonies to
the same cause.   It was no doubt the most forcible and impressive
manner in which they could illustrate the power or grandeur of
their gods.    In fact mimic dances in these early ages, yet
unfashioned by culture, expressed their most intense passions,—
hence the beginning of drama.   Thus dramatic art owes its origin
to religious rites.   We see that it prospered, as well as other arts,
mostly in those countries where idolatry and polytheism have
prevailed.   The Hindu drama and the mysteries of the Middle
Ages are supposed to have had a similar origin.

That this exalted idea of the Deity prevailed among the ancient
Grecian communities cannot be denied.   The Athenians were a
race susceptible of ideal sentiments, loving the beautiful and the

divine. It is not, therefore, to be wondered at that a people, so thoroughly impressed with the traditions of ancestral heroes, should consecrate all that genius could produce, in the shape of art or industry to their gods. All their theatrical performances were, therefore, constituent parts of their religious festivals. This spirit of religion has always been preserved amongst Grecian dramatists, even to the times of Aristophanes, 411 B.C.; Antiphanes, 404 B.C.; Sophocles, 405 B.C. These dramas, which greatly contributed to the amusement and instruction of the people, were at the same time a sacrifice to the Deity. What we have now to see is, how these early festivities gave rise to successive dramatic performances, such as appear in the more perfect dramas and tragedies of Æschylus, born 525 B.C.

The early tragedies were composed of two very distinct parts or modes of composition. The first, a series of choral songs,—*choros*, a word, the original meaning and derivation are somewhat uncertain; according to Homer it means a troop of dancers. The second, dialogues. It is supposed that the choruses had their origin among the Dorians. The choruses were performed at religious festivities or celebrations, when the whole population of a city met to offer up thanksgivings to their guardian gods; they consisted of hymns being sung whilst dances were performed in the *public places*. The Agoma at Sparta was called choros, which would lead to believe that the words *kora* and *komos* would be derived from such places being employed for dancing. These religious ceremonies were held in honour of Apollo; so in the Homeric hymn to the Pythian Apollo a company of goddesses dance, while the muses sing and Apollo plays the cithara or lyre. These were first practised in the Doric states, and music as well as dancing became part of the public education,—among the Spartans especially. Various causes contributed to this, namely, their universal employment in the worship of Apollo,—women taking part in the choral performances. Many dances had a gymnastic character imparted to them, and were employed as a mode of training to martial exercises. Whether these war-dances originated first among the Dorians is doubtful, as it appears that

the Curetes in Crete cultivated the war-dances in honour of Zeus
quite as early as the Dorians practised them in honour of Apollo.
However, as it appears that music and dancing were connected
with the religious, and the political and military organisation of
the Dorians, we might be led to believe that the introduction of
choral poetry into Greece, and the first introduction of instru-
mental music, are due to them.—Apollo was the inventor of the
lyre.—As a proof of this we may notice that the Doric dialect is
preserved in the lyric poetry of the other Grecian tribes, although

REHEARSAL OF A GREEK COMEDY.

there had been other choral-poetry which was not Doric, such as
several Lesbian lyric poems, which appear to have had a choral
character.

The Spartans had three principal dances, the pyrrhic, the
gymnopædic style, and the hyporchematic.*  In all three a certain
amount of mimetic character was displayed, and in the last men-

* Hyporcheme, or choral hymn to Apollo; it was of a lively character,
accompanied with music and pantomimic action.

tioned, especially, the pyrrhic or war dance constituted a portion of the gymnastic and martial training. At the gymnopædia large choruses of men and boys appeared, in which many citizens would take part. It was in the hyporchematic dances that the chorus both sang and danced. The instrument commonly used in connection with the Doric choral poetry was the cithara or lyre. In the pyrrhic dance the flute was employed, and was substituted for the cithara, probably on account of its more piercing tone.* These three dances certainly had their representative in the dramatic poetry of later ages. Athenæus tells us "there are three dances in scenic poetry, the tragic, the comic, and the satyric; and likewise three in lyric poetry, the pyrrhic, the gymnopædic, and the hyporchematic. The pyrrhic corresponds to the satyric, for they are both rapid; the pyrrhic is considered a military dance, for the dancers are boys in armour, and swiftness is needed in war for pursuit and flight. The gymnopædic is similar to the tragic dance which is called emmeleia; a stately tragic measure. Both these dances are conspicuously grave and solemn. The hyporchematic coincides in its peculiarities with the comic dance; they are both full of merriment."

The Dorians who had till then worshipped Apollo as their national deity, as the sun-god, and therefore the chief of a system of elementary religion, adopted Bacchus as the bright and merry god,—this deity they borrowed from their conquered neighbours,—the superintendent of the orphic and black rites, the god of life, also the god of death, as of light. His worship was accompanied by many different kinds of mimicry. Either his sufferings were represented with appropriate wailing accompaniment, or his rites were celebrated with suitable liveliness, as the god of wine, the giver of life. Thus the religion of Bacchus made its way in Greece, and was speedily incorporated with that of the sun-god. This mixed religion became prevalent throughout Greece. The Dorians, then, having a religion with two deities, corresponding, in many respects, with those objects of elementary worship which they found in most of the countries they subdued,

---

* See illustration, page 228.

naturally adjusted their own religion to the similar one already
existing. The earliest species of choral poetry connected with
the worship of Bacchus was called the *Dithyramb*. This ancient
Bacchanalian performance, the origin of which is attributed by
Herodotus to Arion, seems to have been a hymn sung by
one or more of the komos or irregular band of revellers
to the music of the flute. The choruses, which ordinarily
consisted of fifty men or youths, danced in a ring round
the altar of Dionysus,—hence they were called cyclid choruses.
A circular or cyclic chorus was properly any one that was
danced in a ring round an altar, but mostly those appropri-
ated to the worship of Bacchus ; and dithyrambic poets were
understood by the term *kukliodiodidaskaloi*, teachers of the
cyclic chorus. With the introduction of the regular choral
character, Arion also substituted the cithara for the flute.
It is supposed that he invented the *tragic* style, τραγικός τρόπος,
from the fact that he introduced dithyrambs of a gloomy character,
having for their subject the sorrow of Dionysus, as well as the
gayer and more joyous song. Arion is also said to have been the
first to introduce into these choruses satyrs speaking in verses.
Lasus of Hermione gave a freer form to the dithyramb by
divesting it of its antistrophic character, and introducing the
dithyrambic style into compositions not immediately connected
with the worship of Dionysus ; he also introduced caustic jests.
As the dithyramb gradually lost its antistrophic character, it
became more and more mimetic or dramatic ; and as its performances required an increased amount of skill, dithyrambs came
to be performed by educated private persons. As to the chorus
it remained an easy matter, as wealthy men entertained poets
and musicians. But while the dithyramb was thus adopted by
the Dorians, the more primitive forms of worship still existed,—
namely,—the rural celebration of the vintage. From this sprung
the *comedy* of the Greeks ; whilst *tragedy* sprang, as we have
already shown, from the more solemn celebrations of the
dithyramb. What was usually meant by the word—" tragic style "
—may be understood to have been a variation of the dithyramb,

resembling the lyrical tragedy, which is considered an intermediate step between the dithyramb and the regular tragedy.
The lyric drama, although it had yet no actors, still, possessed a
dramatic element, in so far as there were certain *extempore*
effusions of the coryphæi, who related short fables in pantomimic
gesture or language. The term coryphæi or exarchi was applied
to the best dancers in a chorus. The exarchus was either the
best dancer and mimic, or the musician who accompanied the
song on an instrument,—*exarchus* means "the leader." The
exarchus in the dithyramb recited the ode in the first person, and
the chorus danced round the flaming altar. It is therefore
probable that the tragic dialogue had its origin in the speeches of
the leaders in the dithyrambic chorus. Aristotle no doubt spoke
of a near approach to theatrical action, when he states that the
assumption of a mimetic character was the reason why the
dithyramb departed from its originally antistrophic form. In
addition to the choruses and the lyric poetry, attributed to the
Dorians, another kind of entertainment had existed in Greece
from the earliest times, and was considered as peculiar to the
Ionian race. This was the recitation of poems by wandering
minstrels called rhapsodies,—ραψωδοι,—bards who recited epic
poems; probably derived from ραβδos—branch,—as the rhapsodists
chanted in slow recitation, holding a staff in the right hand,
portions of the national epic poetry, which took its rise in the
Ionian States. These rhapsodists recited in iambic verses.
These verses are attributed to Simonides of Amorgus, who is
supposed to have been the first iambic poet (693 B.C.), and are
said by Aristotle to derive their names from their being originally
used for purposes of satire. The word ιαμβιζειν was derived
from ιαμβos,—an iambus—a metrical foot, consisting of a short
and a long syllable, and meant to satirise,—which signification
sprang probably from the frequent use of that species of verse by
Archilochus for the purpose of invective.

There is every probability that the recitation of these poems
was a near approach to theatrical declamation, especially as they
had to be committed to memory, for the means of reproducing
writing at these early times must have been very scanty.

Lord Macaulay, speaking of the opportunities enjoyed by the Athenian for mental culture, says :—" He heard the rhapsodist at the corner of the street, reciting the death of Argus or the shield of Achilles."

The rhapsod, having many occasions to meet in numbers, soon turned their calling into a sort of trade, and accepted engagements to recite certain parts on different solemnities. This they did with great emulation ; and as they sometimes had whole poems from Homer to recite together, each assumed a separate part, which they delivered no doubt with the action of theatrical players.

It is certain that the Athenians took these old iambic poems as models for the dialogues of their tragedies. They adopted the same metre, and often reproduced the very same ideas. The rhapsodist may be considered as the forerunner of the actor, and was indeed almost an actor himself.

It is therefore evident that the union of the Dorian lyric tragedy, and chorus, without actors, and the subsequent tragedy of the Athenian with its rhapsodies, developed in time into the complete and perfect Attic drama.

Thespis, who is said to be the inventor of the Grecian tragedy, was born at Icarius (a Diacrian deme or district), the part of the Ægean between the Cyclades and Caria, where Icarus son of Dædalus, was said to have been drowned. Icarius is also said to have been the seat of the religion of Bacchus, and the origin of the Athenian tragedy and comedy has been referred to the dramatic festivals of the place. Little is known of Thespis. It is supposed, however, that he introduced some alterations into the dances of the chorus. He also introduced an actor into the Dionysian chorus for the sake of variety. As he was an Icarian he worshipped Bacchus ; he probably was also a rhapsodist, and introduced rhapsodical recitations into the Dionysian rites. He is supposed to have invented a compound of herbs to colour the face, and also to have constructed a mask to enable the actor— probably himself—to sustain several characters. To Thespis therefore we are indebted for the further union of the Bacchus and Dionysian celebrations.

Now if we cast a retrospective glance, we find that Dionysus was worshipped by the people of Attica, who formed the tribe of the Ægicores or goat-herds. These goat-herds were conquered by the Ionians, who were worshippers of Bacchus, and were rhapso-dists; and in order to be on an equality with their conquerors, they—in later times—amalgamated their religion with that of the Ionians, and became worshippers of Bacchus. Thus we find the first signs of union between the Dionysian and Bacchic religion, which union was further consolidated by Thespis, who made another important change, by causing the actor or rhapsodist to address his speech to the chorus, which carried on with him through the coryphæus a sort of dialogue. Whilst the chorus stood on the steps of the altar of Bacchus, he was placed on an elevation or table. This may almost be considered as a precursor of the *stage*, since we find that in later times there was always an open space between the thymele, or altar of Bacchus, and the elevated platform whence the actor addressed the public.

Pisistratus, who was the head of the democratical faction, and contemporary with Thespis, greatly encouraged the rhapsodists, and is said to have contributed towards arranging the rhapsodies in their natural and poetic sequence. It is in his time that the union of the rhapsody with the cyclic chorus took place.

Now whether, according to some, the name of Thespis was simply derived from the common epithet of the Homeric minstrel, and implies nothing more in its connection with the history of the drama, it is not in our province to determine; our purpose being simply to show the origin and the develop-ment of the drama, without extending our remarks to historical scrutiny, which would convert this chapter into volumes. To conclude this Thespian period, we may add that the dithyrambic contests took place in a temple built by Pisistratus, in which the victorious choregi used to offer up their sacrifices, which became afterwards a practice between the victors and the tragic chorus.

We have already stated that the comedy of the Greeks arose from the phallic processions, as tragedy originated in the dithy-ramb. How its progress advanced from its primitive rude state to perfection is difficult to settle, yet its origin may be traced in Megara, if we consider that Susarion was the earliest comic poet, and a native of Tripodiscus in Megara. Ancient writers often allude to the coarse humour of the Megarians, and their natural inclination towards the ludicrous. Satiric drama may be considered as the stepping-stone from tragedy to comedy, and is due to the discontent of the people who complained of the serious character of the dramatic exhibitions, and missed the merriment of the country satyrs. This induced Pratinas of Philius,—a contemporary of Æschylus, to write dramas, which, although in the same form as the tragedy, yet had choruses composed of satyrs, and the dances were pyrrhic instead of gymnopædic. Whatever may have been the origin of the Greek comedy, it is evident that it was produced at a country festival in celebration of Bacchus, on which occasions the country people went from place to place in carts, singing songs to their god, also to Phales his comrade, and indulging in jests and speeches of an abusive and satirical type. The word comedy, κωμος, signifies a revel or orgie after supper. It also applied to revellers, who after a banquet, used to parade the streets at night with torches in their hands. This signification can be traced in Æschylus' "Agamemnon," where he says that the Furies, although they had drunk their fill of human blood in the house of Pelopidæ, obstinately stuck to the house instead of departing like κομως. These vintage ceremonies, being of the coarsest kind, formed the most striking part of the rural exhibitions; yet they found their way to Athens when comedy was established at the time of Pericles, as a means used by the demagogues for attacking, with safety to themselves, their political opponents. Thus, public interest having been drawn in this direction, it is supposed that the comic chorus began to stain their faces with the lees of wine as a substitute for masks. We see therefore that tragedy and comedy had a different origin. *Comedy* may be described as a generic cause for dramatic performances which tends to excite laughter; while *tragedy* is an imitation of the noblest life, or of the actions of the gods and heroes. Aristotle says of tragedy, that, by the production of pity and terror it effects the purgation of such passions.* Greek comedy is divided into two kinds,—the old comedy, and the middle comedy. The first was, as we have stated, the successful result of the jests of the country pasquinades, forming part of the Bacchanalian ceremonies, and afterwards used as a means of political sarcasm. Its essence was satire, and the object of general dislike was described in the most abusive terms, and represented on the stage by some one who did the most con-temptible things, and who was turned into ridicule. The middle comedy was an offspring of the older kind, only without a chorus; its character was more literary than political; for this we can account, if we consider that the political strife had temporarily ceased, since the democracy had been overthrown. The old comedy might be termed *caricature*, the middle comedy *criticism*. From these two kinds of comedy originated a third and later one named the new comedy, which dates from the time of Alexander, about a hundred years later than the old comedy. This would correspond to the comic drama of the seventeenth century, which if we take Charles Lamb's definition might be called the comedy of manners. Having thus described the origin of comedy and tragedy, we must pass on to the manner of their performance, without following step by step the different changes and perfecting of the methods of writing by the different Greek poets.

The genius of the Greeks showed itself in tragedy and comedy; and by reading the works of the great dramatists who lived in that period, we see the progressive changes which took place, and the perfecting of these tragedies which were reproduced in later times by the Romans, and which left after them a vacuum of many ages, in the tragic and dramatic exhibitions, before a fresh impetus was given to dramatic writing in Europe.

As we have already stated, the Greek theatre was the temple of the god, and in its centre was the altar dedicated to the

---

* " For buskin'd measures move
Pale grief and pleasing pain,
And horror, tyrant of the throbbing breast."
　　　　　　　　　　　—GRAY, " The Bard."

deity. It was surrounded by steps forming a semicircle, from
which thirty thousand people witnessed the spectacle offered in his
honour. The performances took place in the spring, and lasted
a few days, and every citizen was there from daybreak to sunset.
The theatrical dresses were festive robes worn in the Dionysian
processions. The dramas were adopted or rejected after severe
scrutiny, by a council appointed to decide between the rival
dramatists. The performances formed part of the festivals of
Bacchus. The Attic Dionysia appear to have taken place four
times a year; namely,—in the sixth, seventh, eighth, and ninth
months of the Attic year. These four exhibitions were called,—

1st.   The Country Dionysia ; or, Festival of the Vintage.
2nd.   The Festival of the Wine-press ; or, Lenæa.
3rd.   The Anthesteria ; or, More Ancient Festival of Bacchus.
4th.   The Great Dionysia.

At the first, second, and fourth of these feasts, theatrical exhibitions took place. The performances were conducted according
to their origin, namely, with the chorus and dialogue. The
chorus, at first composed of the whole population, was afterwards,
when arts became more cultivated, entrusted to the care of one
person called the *choragus,* whose duty it was to provide a chorus
for all plays. He had to pay a teacher to train the players in the
songs and dances they had to perform. He was considered as the
religious representative of the whole people ; the whole expense
of the chorus was at his charge. The actors were allotted to the
poet ; the *choragus* had nothing to do with them. The
dramatist was provided with a chorus, and with actors, having to
train the latter. The poet and the choragus united their efforts
and competed for the prize, by a combination of the best taught
actors, and of the most sumptuously dressed and best trained
chorus. That these effects, combined, often redeemed the
weakness of the poem, and influenced the judges in their favour,
is more than probable. The choragus who exhibited the best
entertainment generally received a reward. The place of exhibition was, in the days of the perfect drama, the great stone theatre

erected within the place or ground sacred to Bacchus. It was commenced in the year 500 B.C., and finished about 381 B.C.

The altar of Bacchus round which the cyclian chorus danced, and the stage from which the actor or exarchus spoke,—took the place of the wooden table from which the earlier actors addressed the chorus, and formed the two most important parts of a level space situated twelve feet below the lowest range of seats, enclosed partly by them and partly by the excavations. The altar or platform stood in the middle of this space. Level with the lowest seats of the amphitheatre, or forms, and on the opposite side, stood the platform or stage, constructed partly of wood; the foremost part, for the actor to stand upon when speaking, and partly of stone. The scenery rested on this stony part. The proscenium was backed and flanked by lofty stone buildings, with three entrances upon the proscenium; the chief entrance being an ornamented portal, which was assigned to royalty.*

The scenery corresponded probably to the grandeur of the building. The stage machinery also showed much ingenuity. The gods were seen floating in the air, surrounded by clouds. No doubt a small platform, suspended by means of ropes, served to support and move the celestial beings. Sometimes they would raise a god in the air by means of ingenious contrivances. Thunder was also imitated by using bladders full of pebbles rolled over sheets of copper. There was a place over the stage where the lightning was flashed through clouds. The principal actors were known by the entrance through which they came on the stage.

---

## ROME.

THE exhibitions first introduced in honour of the gods soon almost entirely lost their religious character. During the time of the later republic they had already become the surest means of gaining popular favour. It is related by Dion Cassius, that Augustus having addressed some reproach to Pylades on the

---

* See next illustrations.

THE THEATRE AT EGESTA.

A THEATRE IN ANCIENT GREECE.

subject of that actor's rivalry with one of his companions, Pylades
did not hesitate to answer :—"Cæsar, it is for your benefit that
the people's attention should turn towards us." These public
performances gained great importance, as they afforded the
people the only means of assembling in large numbers, and of
expressing their sympathies and antipathies before their sovereign.
The greeting with which they saluted the monarch on his first
entering the amphitheatre was highly valued by him, and in fact
by all men of high standing.

Chariot races, athletics, combats of gladiators with each other
or with wild beasts, formed the chief recreation of the Romans
for centuries. Already in the earlier times of the Roman
republic, in the year 364 B.C., we find public performances
consisting of chariot races. The exhibitions in the arena had
become almost part of the Roman's education. The people took
as passionate an interest in those spectacles as our young Englishmen in modern games and boat races. We scarcely find in all
the Roman literature any expression of disapproval or horror at
those sanguinary displays. The discussion on the heroes of the
arena supplied a fertile subject of conversation even among the
most learned of the community. These Roman games, as they
were called, extended rapidly through Italy, Greece, Asia Minor,
and to all the oriental countries. The sports that had begun with
chariot races, held in large circuses, degenerated into these
sanguinary games, and the circus made way for the amphitheatre.
The first amphitheatre was built of wood by Julius Cæsar, whose
example was soon followed throughout Spain, Gaul, and Northern
Africa, where almost every large town could boast of an arena,
frequently stained with the blood of countless victims. In Greece
only, where civilisation had reached a higher phase, opposition
was made to the introduction of gladiators; but this objection
was not of long duration, as the king Antiochus Epiphanes, who
was the first to institute these games, encouraged them, and
caused them to become firmly established. This taste for games
of blood was, however, not so generally exhibited as in Rome,
and was found mostly among the lower class. The better

class of people condemned the games of the arena. Plutarch speaks of those games with horror and detestation. Cicero mentions them in the following way :—" What pleasure is it to an educated man to see a weak man torn to pieces by a wild beast of enormous strength, or a beautiful animal pierced by an arrow ? " It is owing to the influence of Christianity that these murderous exhibitions were partly abolished in the year 326. Constantine issued an edict disapproving of " these sanguinary exhibitions that interfere with the calmness of peace," and ordered the work of mimes to be substituted for the games of gladiators. This edict, however, did not long remain in force, for we find Honorius abolishing these games of the arena A.D. 404. In the East these games ceased from the end of the fourth century. They were afterwards revived in a modified form, and the killing of beasts alone was maintained. In the eastern and western countries combats of gladiators to the death continued until the sixth century. In 536 Justinian ordered that wild beast combats should be exhibited amongst other public entertainments. Cassiodorus at the same epoch expressed his admiration at the dexterity and agility with which the wild beast fighters (bestiarii) avoided the attack of ferocious animals, and also at the ingenuity displayed in the means used in defending themselves. Therefore we see that in Rome at this epoch care was taken that the games should be less sanguinary, and that bloodshed should to a certain extent be avoided.

From the beginning of the empire Rome always had three permanent theatres, though all the three together could not contain so many spectators as the large amphitheatre. To counteract the overwhelming excitement of the circus and arena, the stage could only attract the masses by pandering to their low tastes, offering them the bait of laughter and triviality, and lavishing on them coarse entertainments entirely wanting in refinement. Thus instead of counteracting the pernicious effects of sanguinary performances, the theatre contributed to the demoralisation and corruption of the people. The Atellan farce and the "mimus" or mimic plays were the two most popular forms under the

Q

empire. The first, a sort of "Punch" comedy, which originated in Campania, has remained popular even to our own days. It was early established in Rome. A brief action, probably in one act, was carried on by four masked actors, prototypes of characters in the modern comedy of the Italian type. Pappus, the dotard, corresponded to our Pantaloon; Dorsennus, the wise man, alternately a schoolmaster, an ecclesiatic, &c., corresponded to the Dottore; then there was Buccon, the bully or glutton, and Maccus, the fool.

The Atellans that have reached us, although anterior to the empire, make known to us the favourite subjects of this kind, which no doubt remained, under the empire, the same that they had been under the republic. Types of different nationalities were represented, such as Campanians, Transalpine Gauls, Pomatian soldiers, whose peculiar way of speaking and awkward gait must have greatly diverted a city audience. Many titles of these Atellans, such as "Buccon at the Gladiator's School," "Pappus the Countryman," &c., show that the comic situations must have been plentiful. Grotesque and obscene jests were plentifully introduced. The mimic, farce-mimus, was also a characteristic piece taken from ordinary life, short, and without the ordinary masks. It was often given with the Atellan as an interlude or as a supplement after other pieces. It is mentioned as having been most popular. It is the kind of dramatic art that maintained itself longest in public favour; it even survived the fall of the western empire.

The subjects were much the same as the Atellan, and treated more of the urban customs than those of the country, mostly of the inferior classes and artisans. The caricature of foreign nationalities was less marked than in the mimus. Tricks, intrigues, and the chicanery of the law were the subjects most frequently handled. Amorous intrigues also formed part of the entertainment. In the mimus, insults and the representation of plentiful cuffs and kicks administered to simpletons were considered fine points. The language was that in use among the lowest class. The acting was of course on a par with the language, coarse and exaggerated. Buffoonery and grotesque dances formed part of the performance; there were also dances, with accompaniments of flutes. The scenic arrangements were very simple. The mimics performed in front of a stage divided from the back by a curtain. They wore no theatrical shoes or masks. They were dressed in the style of Harlequin, in a kind of coat of different colours, and a cloak. Next to the principal actor or hero of the piece were the fool, and the glutton or parasite, easily recognised by his puffed-out cheeks, bald head, and cringing demeanour. Morality was made the subject of open mockery, and obscenity was paramount; hence the popularity of the works. Women appeared on the stage very scantily clad. Satirical allusions were often made to public affairs, and even to the emperors themselves. Public and actors understood each other, and the allusions made by the latter were eagerly taken up by the audience. The unbridled licence introduced into this kind of entertainment caused the expulsion of the mimes from Italy A.D. 22. Whilst the popular throng took a vivid interest in this class of performances, the classic drama could scarcely be upheld by the restricted circle of learned people. The productive era in tragedy and comedy, although never very great in Italy, but at its best only a reproduction of the Grecian models, had long vanished. The final isolated attempt of this kind was made as far back as the first century of our era. The last pieces that were performed were written under Claudius by L. Pomponius Bassus. Whatever was composed at that time was more suited to the study and private reading. The limited demand for the classic pieces was fully supplied to the stage by the Grecian comedies and tragedies, remodelled for more modern taste. The Palliata, or new Greek comedy, as reproduced by Plautus and Terence in the Roman style, and the Roman comedia togata, maintained themselves in popular favour during the third, and probably the fourth and even the beginning of the fifth, century. The nature of these plays and their tradition required more refined acting, a study of elocution, the modulating of the voice, and a good stage deportment. Roscius was an eminent actor.

Roman actors had a tendency towards realism. Quintilian asserts that he had often seen actors leave the stage in a state of great excitement after moving scenes. In declaiming, they endeavoured to give dignity to the language of ordinary life. Actions were arranged and rendered in accordance with the character of each part.

Among the actors on the Roman stage at the time of Quintilian and Juvenal, the Greeks, "those born actors," as Juvenal called them, chiefly distinguished themselves; Demetrius and Stratocles were the two most celebrated. The former, endowed by nature with a handsome appearance, represented the noble and dignified parts. The latter, with his shrill voice and slender form, was more suited to represent such characters as parasites, slaves, rogues, &c.

Tragedy was even less supported than comedy, but this neglect was not without some cause if we consider the absurd way in which it was represented; strange figures stalking along on the cothurnus or high padded boot, draped in long robes of all colours, decked out with high wigs, and wearing a mask on their face with a large opening at the mouth, which gave them the appearance as though they would swallow the spectators,—all this tended to throw contempt and ridicule on the performance. To give some attraction to the tragedies, splendid scenic effects were added, such as military evolutions executed by horsemen, grand triumphant processions, with foreign and sumptuous dresses; chariots were introduced, and ships, white elephants, giraffes,—in fact, the spectacular part of the performance was so grand, that even the most educated were more attracted by it than by the poet's dramatic work. The consequence was that tragedy soon disappeared, and was replaced, even so far back as the second century, by lyric scenes and pantomimic dances. On the Roman, as well as on the Greek stage, music and dancing formed part of the dramatic expositions. Two persons were engaged in the performance of the dramatic work; the one acted his part by means of a mute dance and pantomimic actions, whilst the other, standing close by him, sang the words appropriate to the gestures of his comrade. Thus all illusion was impossible, and the production of a drama could only be appreciated for its intrinsic merit. This disconnected performance appeared so natural to the Romans, that poets of the time of Pliny invited their friends to hear their poetry recited by people gifted with a more agreeable voice than their own, while the author accompanied certain words of the reciter with appropriate gestures and varieties of facial expression.

This separation of the elements which composed tragedy—singing and dancing—diminished the already waning taste for tragedy, and gave an impetus to the other two branches. The

SCENE FROM A ROMAN COMEDY.

pantomimic performances acquired a very great importance, and the pantomimic action was considered of more consequence in the drama than the declamation and singing. This may be explained by the fact that the tragedian, who appeared fully dressed and with his features concealed by a mask, could only supply the want

of facial expression by the significant activity of his gestures :—
moreover, this kind of illustration of different passions and
impersonations on the part of the tragedians was thoroughly
appreciated by a mass of people who understood neither Latin
nor Greek, and no doubt contributed to the establishment of
pantomimes.

The mimic dances were greatly improved under Augustus,
and pantomimic dramas soon replaced tragedy. A single pantomimist executed several lyric solos, taking the parts of various
male and female characters, whilst the text relating to each part
was sung no longer by a single singer but by a chorus.

Distinguished poets composed texts for their ballets, and sold
them to the dancers. These texts generally had a mythological
character. Pylades introduced the innovation of a chorus instead
of the single singer, and also an orchestra composed of cymbals,
guitars, lyres, flutes, and reed pipes ; time was kept by the
*scabillum*, a sort of pedal made of two plates, attached to the foot,
and which knocked against each other at each stamp of the foot.
Two kinds of pantomimes were recognised, the one attributed to
Alexandrinus Bathyllus, the other to the Cicilian Pylades. The
former kind of pantomime was mostly extracted from satiric
subjects, the latter derived from tragedy.

The Grecian dance called the pyrrhic was also represented on
the stage. Apuleius has fully described these pyrrhic and mythological dances, which remind us of the modern ballets.

Diocletian was, it seems, the first who abolished the law that
fixed dishonour on all who had appeared on the stage during their
minority, and excluded them from all high offices. By the
Julian law, senators and all their representatives were prohibited from marrying the sons or daughters of an actress. A
soldier who turned actor incurred the penalty of death. An art
thus branded by society was practised only by slaves, or by freed-
men or foreigners,—such as Greeks, Orientals, or Egyptians,
amongst whom the Roman prejudice did not exist.

The families of slaves in wealthy houses comprised not only
pantomimists, but also comedians, tragedians, and whole troops of

actors. They could be transferred, by gift, from one master to another. Sometimes they obtained their enfranchisement through their talent, although on their emancipation they bound themselves to hold themselves at the disposal of their master whenever he wanted them for himself or his friends, and to perform gratis for him. This degraded condition of the actor did not, however, prevent some distinguished artists from obtaining most brilliant positions, and earning great fortunes by their art. Some became great favourites of the emperors, and were even invested with titles.

Paris, a celebrated pantomimist, who was condemned to death by Domitian, had the following epitaph composed for him by Martial :—" Traveller, who wendest on this Flaminian road, pass not carelessly by, before this noble monument of marble. The delight of Rome, the wit of Alexandria ; art, grace, humour, joy ; the ornament, the sorrow of the Roman stage ; all the goddesses and gods of love,—lie buried in this tomb." This love for the stage caused great emulation amongst the actors, who vied with each other in the endeavour to gain public favour and to secure the suffrage of patrons, and persons were distributed over the theatre to applaud the actors. The rivalry between Pylades and Bathyllus in the year 17 B.C. already caused great disorders in the theatre, but Augustus humoured the two actors, who thus diverted public attention from political affairs.

Scenes of combat and bloodshed became so frequent, that Tiberius banished from Italy actors who had been the cause of those troubles. Nero, on the other hand, in the year 55, withdrew the pretorian cohorts who had the duty of guarding the theatre, and not only allowed party strife, but himself headed one of the parties, and in one of these melée fights he himself threw a projectile which wounded a pretorian in the head. The pantomimists, who were considered the chief instigators of these disorders, were again forbidden to appear on the stage ; but in 106 and afterwards, without intermission, they were allowed to practise their art unmolested. It was customary for many pantomimists to take up the name of their celebrated predecessors, or to be so called by their masters, as a mark of consideration.

Thus the names of Paris, Pylades, Bathyllus, are often read of in the annals of the Roman theatre.

The first Paris was a favourite of Nero, and died by the torture A.D. 67; the second lived at Domitian's court, and was known by the epithet of Paris, already mentioned by Martial; the third lived in the reign of Lucius Verus; the fourth is known by a medal; and the fifth is mentioned by Antiochus. Memphius, Apolaustus (pantomimist), Theocritus (a dancer), Favor Labitius, Urbicus, were all favourite names amongst the actors and lyric artists. Æmilius Glapyrus figured amongst the harpist-singers.

We see so far the connection between the Grecian and the Roman theatre. We will now, although more briefly, trace the history of the stage as it approaches our modern times. With the Christian era began the reactionary influence which gradually drew away the morbid taste from sanguinary displays and strife, and attracted the people to more humane and Christian ideas. In the end of the second century, Tertullian, one of the fathers of the Church, wrote a treatise, "*De Spectaculis,*" denouncing the lovers of plays,—in which the features, hair, age, sex, sighs, laughter, are all false,—as unworthy of the kingdom of God, who loves truth. He quotes Lycurgus, who would not tolerate the theatre in Sparta; and Solon, who is reported to have said, on seeing the car of Thespis, " Are you not ashamed to tell so many lies?"* The Church combated on the one hand the passionate love for the performance of paid Roman actors ; on the other, the indifference displayed for human life in the amphitheatre, where Christians often were thrown into the arena as a prey to the wild beasts. Although Christianity had triumphed over the Greek gods, yet it proved powerless to put down the performance of dramatic plays inculcated by the Romans. During the Middle Ages, all the various periods, even the most barbarous, have added a page to

---

* Latin comedy fell gradually into decay, and died out with the ruin of the Roman empire and the invasion of the barbarians, and until the time of Charlemagne no trace is left of the theatre in Italy.

the history of the stage,—from the fourth century, which gave us the suffering Christ, until the tenth, when Roswitha, the nun, from Sandersheim, endeavoured by her Christian pieces to destroy the ancient theatre. Nor could Christianity annul the Grecian influence which gave rise to the tragedy of the "Passion of Christ," ascribed to Gregory Nazienzen, who was called by his contemporaries the great lyric poet of the Greek Church.

Christian literature at that time was a mixture of old Greek and modern Christian material fused into one mould. In the "Passion of Christ," as it was performed by the Christians of the fourth century, the action takes place behind the scenes, and is only announced by messengers,—the principal actress being the Virgin mother, who represents and illustrates the sufferings of her Son; and although her lament is not devoid of pathos, the verses are diffuse and long drawn out. The "Passion of Christ," the first Christian drama, has its foundation in Attic tragedy. It was owing partly to the Church's contention against the theatre that the handsome buildings for all sorts of amusements were allowed in the fifth century to fall into ruin. They were utilised afterwards as quarries, whence were drawn the materials for castles and cathedrals. Actors, however, never disappeared entirely, but appeared as *jongleurs*, players, mummers, who no doubt were a degenerate offspring of the Roman actors. They held exhibitions of mummery in the streets and at public festivals. Sometimes they were tolerated, in order to amuse the people; at other times they were driven away as vagabonds. The mass at the time of Gregory the Great was a dramatic celebration, full of religious emotion. In the procession that took place in the different towns, generally in commemoration of a saint, and later in the pageantries of Corpus-Christi day, very striking religious mummeries were performed by priests, friars, corporations, &c., in their various picturesque costumes, with togas and banners. Adam and Eve were represented, carrying the tree of knowledge; St John the Baptist appeared as a herald, carrying the banner of Christ and a lamb; Judas, bearing a bag of money, followed by the devil with the gallows; and various saints, according to their individuality. In France, Germany, and Italy, pageants of a less religious kind were held in honour of some hero. The first record of the development of the miracle-play is found in France, in the eleventh century, and its example was soon followed in all German and Latin nations. The "*Rise and Fall of Antichrist*," an Easter play of the twelfth century, is the first great miracle-play which we possess of German origin. The scenic arrangement was very simple, and from its description we may infer that it was a musical play intended to be performed. The scenery is thus given:—In the background, facing the east, is the temple of the Lord; in front of it, the thrones of the principal personages surrounded by their armies. The intercourse between the princes sitting on their thrones is carried on by messengers, and the space is supposed to be large enough to represent the distance between Germany and Jerusalem. Allegorical personages open the play. Pagans and Jews appear as women. The Church is represented in kingly crown and armour, accompanied by Mercy with the olive branch, and Justice with the balance and sword; and is followed, on the right, by the Pope and clergy, on the left by the Emperor and his hosts. The kings of the earth bring up the rear. In the first part the emperor sends heralds to the kings of the earth to demand submission. The French king claims the right of supremacy, and not until he loses the battle does he submit. The emperor's aid is then claimed by the King of Jerusalem to defend the Church against the King of Babylon and Paganism. The emperor crushes them, and deposits the crown of Babylon in the temple of the Lord. In the second part of the play Antichrist appears, wearing a short mail hidden under his wings; Hypocrisy and Heresy stand one on each side of him, and try to win the king's favour; he, however, sees through the intended deception, and subdues the army of Antichrist. The latter personage, however, works miracles, heals a cripple and a leper, and brings to life a man who has *feigned death*. He once more regains his power; but shortly after a sound is heard from above,—*Antichrist falls*. The hypocrites rush away; and all return to the true faith, and the Church rejoices. Then she receives her own again, and sings, "Praise ye the Lord."

From the thirteenth century the miracle-play, as it severed itself gradually from the Church offices, was banished from the churches by the Popes, as being connected more or less with profane amusements. These miracle-plays, till then performed in Latin, drifted into the vulgar tongue with the acting of the people. Occasionally lay brethren assisted in the pious work. In Antwerp, a brotherhood—St Luke's—consisting mostly of artists and artificers, acted the old Flemish pieces ; and in Paris, the Confrérie de la Passion, composed of artisans, received from Charles VI., in 1402, a charter for the exclusive performance of miracle-plays in the towns and suburbs. In Rome, the brotherhood *Del Gonfalone* played in passion week the sufferings of Christ, in the Colosseum, once the very arena where so many Christians were torn to pieces by wild beasts.

Sometimes a whole town would take part in the play. In that case a *trumpet call* summoned all, and each one had to sign a document and swear under penalty of death to study carefully his part. Such performances took place in the open air, on a very large stage; and as scenic decorations were unknown, the different places where a town, house, or forest ought to have been, were indicated by a written inscription, the names being affixed on a board. In France, and also in England, there was often a stage with three stories ;—to represent paradise, the upper stage was adorned with tapestry and trees ; then the earth the middle stage : and hell the lower part. In Germany, paradise was only at one end of the stage raised a few steps from the rest ; the devil had for his abode a large cask. The actors being invisible, some one on the stage indicated by a dumb show whence the noise came, either from paradise or from earth. When the actors made their first appearance, they, or some one for them, had to state what each one represented. These miracle-plays, as already stated, degenerated gradually into cynical speeches and mere orgies, and were prohibited from time to time by Gregory IX., the Council of Treves in 1227, William Waddington in the thirteenth century, William of Wykeham in 1384; but all was in vain. These miracle-plays kept their popularity for five centuries, and were still in vogue

EARLY DRAMA: A MIRACLE PLAY.

in the time of Shakespeare. The " Chester Mysteries " were performed in 1567 and 1574; however, they were finally suppressed after four days' performance. They began from the time of the Norman conquest, and are mentioned as familiar spectacles by Matthew Paris and Fitzstephen in the very beginning of the twelfth century. Protestantism had no small share in destroying the superstitions and the abuses of an exhibition which did not coincide with its sober faith. At Eisenach, after Easter 1322, when the country was at peace, a play of the "*Wise and Foolish Virgins*" was acted before the Landgrave Frederick "of the bitten cheek." Seeing that the foolish virgins found no mercy, although Mary herself interceded for them, the Landgrave exclaimed,— " What sort of faith is Christian faith, if Christians cannot be pardoned even at the intercession of the mother of God and all the saints ? "

## MORALITIES.

IF religion was taught by the mysteries, philosophy was taught by the moralities. Thus this branch of education was made popular. In mediæval times Latin dissertations were written for the learned, whilst for the mass the subjects of education were treated as dramas. The first allegoric characters were Faith, Hope, and Charity; virtues and vices also appeared as personages.

In the Middle Ages allegory and fable are found simultaneously. The old fable writers remained popular, as they gave a sparkling form to the aphorisms and maxims which at that time passed for wisdom. Allegory facilitated the study of moral questions. Latin treatises were cut into pieces, and human sentiments were personified and appropriately dressed. So soon as morality detached itself from religion, allegory filled the pages of literature ; sometimes it gives birth to graceful poems, at others it takes the shape of animals performing human actions, the story in each case inculcating a moral. Occleve, Gower, Heywood, and others

wrote lengthy and often heavy poems, such as Heywood's "The
Spider and the Fly" (1556). It is a long tale in verse. The fly
represents the Catholics, and is caught in the web of the spider
—image of the Protestants. After numerous quarrels and alterca-
tions, the servant—or queen—kills the spiteful spider. The
whole story was so diffuse, that Harrison said :—"The author has
displayed such depth and learning, that neither himself nor those
who read the book can rise to its level." The theatrical pieces
derived from the same sort of ideas are obscure in their meaning,
devoid of interest, and always end with a moral. A few sublime
ideas only are found scattered among endless and grotesque
maxims of classical, philosophical, and theological reminiscences.
The very basis of the play is anti-dramatic. In the morality the
personage is determined beforehand, and often describes himself
whether he is a vice or a virtue ; his acts, deeds, and answers are
all fixed beforehand. From the first scene all know what is to
follow, and the inevitable moral result, namely, the triumph of
virtue and sobriety over vice and dissipation. Most of these
dramas are stereotyped in this form. The piece generally begins
with a monologue, in which the speaker describes himself either
as Wisdom, Nature, &c. A man comes and announces that he
believes in God, but has no decided tendency either towards
good or evil. Then Sensuality, Innocence, Justice. Virtue, all vie
with each other to win the man's heart. Sensuality and his
friends take this man to the harem, which is there to represent
all dissipation and crimes. The man, after a good deal of
sporting and flirting with "Nell, the pretty dancer," or "Bess, the
jolly lass," repents, seeks his wise and virtuous friends, and the
piece ends with a benediction. Such is the nature of the moralities
called the "Interlude of Youth;" "Nature;" "The Four Elements,"
&c. (1555). Vice is almost always represented as the buffoon of the
piece ; he is armed with a wooden sword or dagger, and is always
very popular. The "Interlude of the Four Elements" (1510) is a
philosophical drama, in which science and mathematics are inter-
polated. The lark, for instance, is suspended in the middle of the
firmament ; the rain, thunder, snow, meteors, are fully explained.

Nature opens the play, and describes himself in the most elaborate manner. Humanity listens, then Sensuality comes in and takes him to the tavern. Then follows a sort of geographical description. The *World* and *Nature* seemed to be favourite personages. Hence Medwall, chaplain to the Archbishop of Canterbury, wrote "A goodly enterlude, copylyd by master Henry Medevall, chaplayn to the ryht Rev. Father in God Johan Morton somtyme Cardynall and Archbyshop of Canturbery, 1538."

"NATURE.

"There ys in erthe no maner thynge
That ys not partyner of my influence :
Who taught the cok hys watche houŕes to observe,
And sing of corage wyth shryll throte on hye ?
Who taught the pellycan her tender heart to carue ?

.     .     .     .     .     .     .

Certes I nature and none other wyght."

These allegories, however, were heavy and tedious. Collier in his history of English dramatic poetry tells us that Henry VIII., who was present at one of Medwall's moralities, found it so dull, in spite of the renowned buffoon, that he left the room suddenly.

Magnificence,—"Magnyfycence,"—a goodly interlude by Mayster Skelton, 1531, and other pieces of his, were extremely popular.

The authors of moralities wanted to propagate their doctrines, and did so by means of the theatres, which were popular; thus they preached in the form of dialogues to those who would not have gone to church. The comic, coarse, and laughable parts were assigned to the bad propensities. All these moralities, as time went on, drifted more and more towards the comedy of characters, but before true comedy had attained its perfect form. The farce was the natural consequence of the moral dramas, and the stepping-stone from moralities to comedy. Some comedies, however, appeared between these progressive attainments, and borrowed from both of the two styles their most refined qualities. Thus was composed the admirable comic play, "Gammer Gurton's Needle, a ryght pithy, pleasaunt, and merie comedie, played on stage not longe ago in Christes College in Cambridge, made by Mr S., Master of Art,* London, 1575," Elizabethan period. In France the *farce* attained its full maturity —beneath the mantle of the mystery—in the fifteenth century.

## FARCE.

ON Shrove Tuesday, 1511, was acted a play called "The Prince and Mother of Fools," composed by Gringore, herald of the court of Lorraine : "Le jeu du prince des sots et mère sotte, mis en rime francaise par Pierre Gringore et joué par personnaiges aux Halles de Paris le Mardy gras de l'année 1511." In this play holy Mother Church, wearing a triple crown, acknowledges with brazen frankness that she has been guilty of many tricks attributed to her by the *reformed*. On suspicion that she is not the true church, her vestments are torn off, and the mother of the fools is discovered. About the same time we read in Gil Vincente, a Portuguese poet, of a seraph introduced into a play performed at a public fair in honour of the Virgin. The seraph offers to sell the fear of God to the Pope and the clergy by weight, and as the devil protests, Mercury shows up the conduct of Holy Rome, who dispenses the salvation of souls for a remuneration.

## POLEMIC PLAYS.

DURING the carnival, when all joined in jest and indulged in more or less humorous recreation, jokes and satire on the Papacy, which often led to the most serious religious controversy, were hidden under the cloak of the licence of the time and place. Such jesting seemed to be most popular, and at the same time less liable to punishment. In Berne, in 1522, Niclaus Manuel had his play, "The Devourer of the Dead," represented in the

---

* John Still, afterwards Bishop of Bath and Wells.

Kreuzgare by some of his Bernese friends. It was a satirical morality, based on the taking of money for masses for the dead by the clergy. These farces or satirical dramas show the beginning of the estrangement of the people from the clergy, and in same degree a movement towards reformation,—hence the name of "polemic plays." The Catholic retort to these was perhaps not so prolific in dramatic performances, yet offered many counterparts of them; for instance, Luther and his wife, Katherine of Bora, the nun, are brought to disgrace, and the Reformation is represented as a tissue of lies, &c.

Philip II. ordered the commemoration of the massacre of St Bartholomew by a festival play called "The Triumph of Faith." Sir David Lindsay, the Scottish "Lyon King at Arms," was foremost amongst the nobles who chiefly contributed to the reformation of the old faith. Born in 1490, he was at the court of James V. of Scotland, entertaining the monarch with his verses and songs, and by dancing and singing, accompanying himself on the lute. He was outspoken, and undertook to reform the theatre. In his satire on "The Three States"—a poem on the three classes—he represents Scotland and all its orders of society, from the beggar to the king, and passes in review its abuses;—representing the king himself as accessible to flattery and given to various vices. This work forms a very long drama, in which he brings forward a large number of personages, including buffoons, who render the satire general. It was represented for the first time in 1535, and again in 1539, before the king and queen, and the whole court, at the special request of the king; and in 1554, before the queen-regent, on which occasion it played nine hours. Although the religious reform in England and Scotland was making rapid strides, yet it had not had any direct influence on literature. It is not until the time of Cromwell and the Puritans that the Bible became *the book*.

The theatres were closed, and dramas ceased to be written. It is not until after the Restoration that actors reappeared on the stage. The theatre had then lost its former originality; the habits and ideas of the nation had drifted into a new channel, and imitations of French writers, with an extraordinary amount of licence and looseness in thought and language, prevailed until the revival of Shakespeare rescued the English stage from its decay. To the farces and polemic as well as theological dramas must be added the *interludes*, which may be considered the connecting link between the morality and the true drama. In the days of Henry VIII. interludes were a part of literature. They consisted in representing in action, jests, or serious thoughts ; and formed part of entertainments given by the nobility and gentry to their friends. These interludes were performed during or after a banquet, and in large households, and often by the servants of the mansion themselves, by those especially who were gifted with aptitude for mimicry. John Heywood, who excelled in this kind of literature, wrote an interlude in one act called "The Four P's ; namely, a Palmer, a Pardoner, a Poticary, and a Pedlar." These parts were taken by four servants, and performed during a banquet. The action turns upon a trial of skill among the four as to which of them will tell the greatest lie.

PALMER.

" Now say thy worst ;
   Now let us hear of all thy lies,
   The greatest lie thou may'st devise,
   And in the fewest words thou can."

POTICARY.

" Forsooth, you are an honest man."

PEDLAR.

"There said he much, but yet no lie."

POTICARY.

"If we both lie, and you say true,
   Then of these lies your part adieu."

Then follows the narration of extravagant tales.

PEDLAR.

" That each of you one tale shall tell ;
   And which of you tell'th most marvèl,
   And most unlikest to be true,
   Shall most prevail whate'er ensue."

The Pardoner and the Poticary each tell an extravagant tale, and the Palmer caps it by expressing his astonishment at Satan's finding women so troublesome :—

> "Whereby much marval to me ensueth,
> That women in hell such shrews can be,
> And here so gentle, as far as I see.
> Yet have I seen many a mile,
> And many a woman in the while.
> No one good city, town, or borough,
> In christendom, but I've been through ;
> And in this I would ye would understand
> I have seen women five hundred thousand,
> And oft with them long time have tarried.
> Yet in all places where I have been,
> Of all women that I have seen,
> I never saw nor knew, in my conscience,
> Any one woman out of patience."

### POTICARY.

" By the mass there is a great lie."

### PARDONER.

"I never heard greater, by our Lady."

### PEDLAR.

" A greater ! nay, know ye any so great ?"

So the prize is awarded to the Palmer for having told the biggest lie.

We see by another interlude, entitled "A New Enterlude, printed in 1573, no less wittie than pleasant, entituled New Custom," that it was written for ten people, but arranged so as to be played by four only. The parts were as follows :—

1. Perverse Doctrine.

2. { Ignoraunce.
     Hypocrisie.
     Edification.

3. { New Custome.
     Avarice.
     Assurance.

4. { Light of the Gospel.
     Creweltie.
     Godde's felicitie.
     The Prologue.

Coarse jokes, as we see, are introduced in these *interludes* and *moralities*. They were not true plays; and although it cannot be said that the true drama derived its direct source from them, yet the taste for such entertainments developed, in the houses of the rich and of the lords, a taste for the encouragement of skilled actors. From the castle, talent migrated into more humble abodes, and soon was welcomed by the people at large, who took delight in exhibitions that touched upon questions in which all felt more or less interest; and when the drama at last appeared, it found companies of actors ready to interpret it.

If we cast a rapid glance backward at the origin of the theatre in the *Flemish* countries, we find that, as in the Greek theatre, it had its foundation in religion. We see that in the most remote times the liturgic ceremonies, and the archery meetings, gave birth respectively to the *mysteries* and to the *moralities*. The clergy were the first to take part in religious and dramatic exhibitions,— the priests spread the knowledge of the holy history by means of scenic representations. In the twelfth century the mysteries were performed in the church and churchyard, on occasions of great religious festivals, such as the birth of our Saviour, the resurrection, &c.

The local festivities were the occasions for the performance of plays in honour of certain patron saints. All those celebrations which were originated by the priests were after a time extended to the laymen, who became the performers; thus they degenerated into a sort of mingled work of profane and sacred drama, and at length were forbidden in 1293 by the synodal statutes of Utrecht. These performances thus migrated from the church into the street; and not only was the passion celebrated with the display of a scenic performance, but in 1405, at Oudenarde, pantomimic representations were given, with the employment of inscribed rolls containing religious maxims and allegories. The shooting guilds also performed dramatic pieces, with kings, syndics, buffoons, banners,—in fact, a complete pageant. The members of these guilds were called "Gesellen" (companions), and took the opportunity of these meetings to give exhibitions where coarse jokes and buffoonery formed the principal attraction.

The origin of the chambers of rhetoric and literary societies are attributed to the "Gesellen," who were engaged by the companies of the archers to enliven their solemnities by those scenic games and festivities, which lasted several days. The number of spectators who attended these meetings must have been very great, as also the number of performances, if we judge by the following verses found in Martin le Franc's poem "L'Adversaire" :—

> " Va-t-en aux festes à Tournay,
> A celles d'Arras et de Lille,
>   D'Amiens, de Douay, de Cambray,
> De Vallenciennes, d'Abbeville :
>   Là Verras-tu des gens dix mille
> Plus qu'en la forêt de Iorfolz,
>   Qui servent par sales, par viles,
> A ton dieu, le prince des folz."

From 1428 to 1562 important festivities took place every year in different towns, when the monotony of archery meetings was relieved by the performances of the Gesellen, and latterly by theatrical performances. Not only the town but also the country people took part in these exhibitions, which were kept up until the year 1764, when at Petegem was represented the martyrdom of St Mark, and at Marcellin of St Sebastian, patron of the town, who lived in the time of the Roman emperor Diocletian. These Gesellen formed themselves into associations or societies, which became either scientific or dramatic. A rhetorical society, called the "Mother-Society of Ypres," was formed; being the oldest, and invoking the protection of the Holy Trinity, it enjoyed privileges, rights, and authority over other societies, who could not be established without its consent, and who had to submit all their by-laws and regulations to the mother society. The members of these societies had their blasores, also their chiefs, who were called princes, emperors, deans, &c. ; a fiscal to maintain order, a standard-bearer, and a buffoon were also appointed. In the smaller societies one person fulfilled two functions.

The buffoons used to play a very important part in the farces that were performed during the processions of the "Holy Sacrament." They often accompanied the magistrates, who kept them in their own service or retinues. Even to this day the practice—five centuries old—of introducing a clown in the shooting assemblies is still kept up. On the eve of a shooting match, a fifer, drummer, and clown go and greet the members of the brotherhood. The clown performs a dance before their house, and presents them with a small blazon mounted with a quill feather, which the sportsman ties carefully to his coat.

Religious disputes gave rise to the ridiculous and farcical performances of the mysteries; and the satire, irony, and violent vituperations against religious sects, caused Philip II. to issue an edict in 1559 forbidding the performance of any comedy without special authority. In the sixteenth century the rhetorical societies were dispersed, and with them disappeared the performance of these comedies. Alva and his accomplices ruined Belgium; its national character, its democratic habits, were destroyed, and the country was overrun with monks, priests, and courtiers. Although most of the rhetoricians had taken refuge in foreign lands, the theatre recovered from its temporary ruin; but it was placed in the hands of the clergy. Dramatic plays were performed in ecclesiastical schools, conducted by Jesuits, Oratorians, Augustins,—a theatre belonged to the establishment, and the whole dramatic action, with continuous scenery and allegorical ballets, was represented. A sort of rivalry arose among the different institutions, and in order to attract the pupils they issued carefully prepared bills. The comic element was not in any way introduced, as we may judge by the following programme :—" Fête in honour of Monseigneur Francois de Vaulabelle, Bishop of St Omer, by the students of the Society of Jesus, 1511 ; the angel of the church of St Omer will dance a ballet, and the angel of the church of St Omer will gambol at the end of every symbolic drama as a true son of Terpsichore."

## SACRED DRAMA IN SPAIN.

An offspring of the mysteries during the fifteenth century, and probably more of the moralities, had been the "Autos," acts or deeds. Thus we read of "Autos and Nascimiento," or Christmas plays. In Madrid, festive dances accompanied the procession of the Corpus Christi through the streets, a stuffed giant and an immense snake being carried as symbols of paganism. A company of strolling actors travelled from place to place to act the "Autos Sacramentales," or sacred deeds. In the towns a scaffolding was erected on wheels, and surrounded by three small houses of varied colours, and brought there for the occasion. They served as dressing-rooms for the actors, and also as a means of extending the stage. These actors used to travel after a performance, probably without changing their dress, so as to arrive at their next destination in good time, especially when they were going to perform in a country place where no scaffolding or stage would be needed. Thus we see a company of actors described as sitting in a cart, and going to act the "auto" of "Las Cortes de la Muerte," the Court of Death :—a man dressed as Death ; Cupid, an angel with large wings ; a man in armour ; and an Emperor, with a tinsel crown,—the cart being driven by a horrible Devil. The performances took place in the daytime, tapers being lighted in honour of the Deity. The actors acted the "Corpus Christi" play, impersonating allegorical attributes,—Light, Darkness, the Church, &c. Many "autos sacramentales" were composed by Lope de Vega and Calderon. In the auto of "Psyche," by the latter author, we see mythology mixed with Christianity. Both these poets wrote most admirable "autos," Calderon especially ; for with him (1600 to 1681), died the sacred drama and the poetry of the time, and into each he infused a sublimity of sentiment and a fervour which made it truly national poetry. He added popularity to his works by intermingling in them the comic element. Next to the mysteries and "autos" were the lives of the saints, which ministered to the popular craving for the miraculous. Although much decried by Cervantes, these sacred dramas were considered as the more powerful means of awakening in a people already predisposed to fanaticism a profound sense of religious feeling. They were performed in the theatre by professional actors, who no doubt were themselves the offspring of strolling players who had taken part in the ancient mummeries. In Lope de Vega's religious dramas the truth and abuse of religious doctrines are fully represented. It is said that Don Juan was introduced into a drama called the "Atheist Struck Down," which would show that the secular element was gradually introduced into religious dramas. An amusing tale is told of Calderon, who had to perform the part of Adam, Philip IV. representing the Creator. Whilst describing the beauties of paradise he perceived that the king was growing impatient, and asked what was the matter. "What is the matter?" cried Philip, "I grieve at having created such a long-winded Adam!" Calderon and Lope de Vega's dramas are mostly religious and religious polemics; both attacked Protestantism with hatred, as may be seen in the former's "Schism of England."

---

## TRAGEDY AND COMEDY IN THE XIIItH AND XIVtH CENTURIES IN FRANCE.

THE history of French comedy may be traced from the thirteenth century, and although it presents different tendencies and shows various periods, it never deviated entirely from its original form and traditions, from its commencement to our days. Tragedy, on the contrary, may be said to have passed almost suddenly, without any intermediate gradations, during the age of the "Renaissance," from the mystery to the classical tragedy. Although in the year 1568 such dramas as "Paul le Furieux; tragédie prise de la Bible, faite selòn l'art à la mode des vieux poêtes tragiques," were represented, still, as is indicated by the title, these dramas followed antique models. The classic theatre of our modern time differs from that of olden times in the conception of the drama and scenic effects, the interest resting on the development of an intrigue or situation. A tragic situation is based on the conflict of contrary passions, displayed and interwoven by the combination of different incidents, leaving the spectator doubtful as to the issue, and rouses his curiosity by unforeseen complications. Modern melodrama, no doubt, often carries these complications to a degree which passes all the bounds of common sense and probability. The theatre of the Middle Ages was very different; instead of carrying on intrigue in an intricate manner, and ending it in an ingenious way, its object was to make a spectacular display; and instead of representing the deepest and most hidden passions of the soul, it gave a more superficial aspect of an action which was carried on by a large number of actors, without limit of time or place, either in heaven, earth, or hell, a few verses separating two centuries, or a few yards representing a distance of a thousand miles. The old theatres represented everything simultaneously; the modern theatre shifts its scenery, and each scene represents a room, a palace, or a limited tract of country. The ancients, on the contrary, imagined they saw a world in each different part of the stage. The old theatre was based on the superstitious predilection for the marvellous, the whole action soaring into the supernatural. On the contrary, in the modern theatre, the classical drama, reasoning and metaphysical, admits of no superhuman incidents. In the Middle Ages, the characters, if any, are weak; all the personages can almost be compared to bas-reliefs, scarcely delineated, without any perspective, but grouped on the same plan without harmony. The mystery admitted of comicalities and buffoonery; these elements were side by side with the sublime. The scenes that composed it were supernatural, realistic, and trivial; instead of the elegant, noble, and powerful style which prevails throughout modern tragedy.

Although the mysteries were badly written, yet they were spontaneously created by the people themselves. They had taken root in their habits and belief; nothing in them was factitious or borrowed, and for this reason they were immensely popular. Our classic tragedies, on the contrary, are appreciated only by the smaller number, comprising the educated class. In the Middle Ages, the play resembled the Grecian drama, inasmuch as it glorified the Deity, the saints, and the martyrs, as the Greek tragedy had set forth the power and sway of the gods. The Renaissance, however, would not see this, and, banishing religion as well as all comic elements, and even the history of the present, turned for inspiration to the Greeks and Romans. Corneille was the first to promote this imitation of the antique tragedy, embellishing his subject with the sublimity of his sentiments and his scholastic treatment. In his " Polyeute " he exalts the heroism of Christian martyrdom, without being influenced in any degree by the "mysteries." He dramatised St Polyeuctus, and made it still more palatable to the state of the time by introducing a woman, whose heart is divided between her newly married husband and her lost lover, to whom she had successfully opposed her virtue. In 1669 the Germans represented Polyeuctus, showing a vivid reminiscence of the mysteries, by introducing idols which were destroyed, and crucifying the Christians in sight of the audience, and the gates of heaven and hell were opened. Racine wrote " Esther " for the Demoiselles de St Cyr, basing his drama on the Scriptural book of Esther, and shortly afterwards he produced " Athalie,"—Athaliah, the daughter of king Ahab of Israel. This tragedy, which met with much opposition, was pronounced after the death of Racine (1699), the greatest work of the greatest French tragic poet. "Athalie" was also written for the Demoiselles de St Cyr, but never performed in their institution. "Zaire" was written by Voltaire in 1732, and was called the "Christian Tragedy;" but we know that Voltaire had no particular sympathy with Christianity, which he only introduced in order to exhibit a difference of religion as an obstacle to the union of the lovers.

## ORIGIN OF THE FRENCH COMEDY.

THE history of the French comedy, unlike the serious drama, was not divided into distinct periods by the Renaissance.

Between the mediæval mystery and the modern tragedy there is nothing in common, the versification, style, and scenery are all changed. Comedy, on the contrary, shows no interruption, no thorough change after its first origin. From the thirteenth century to our own time, a steady development, with slow modifications, always of a similar literary form, can be observed. Thus, on this ground, the perfection of the comic style can be explained. The traditions have been handed down for six centuries, and reached Molière, who boasted of taking his subject-matter where he found it, " de prendre son bien partout où il le trouvait." It was said that " ses vols étaient des conquêtes " ; at any rate, such material as had accumulated for centuries was a legitimate inheritance, which his great genius has worked out in an unrivalled style. The origin of French comedy is unknown. Probably the jongleurs (jugglers), from the time of the Capetian dynasty, possessed a vast collection of satires and buffoonery ; but no trace of this is left, and no text of any comedy is supposed to have been written until the thirteenth century, when a short piece, " Le Garçon et l'Aveugle " is mentioned, and bears a great analogy with the farces. It is from the reign of Charles VI. (1380 to 1422), that we can trace the origin of the farces, moralities, " sotties," monologues, jovial sermons, which developed into full dimensions in the modern ages, in the course of two centuries. Comedy, however, existed in a different form at the time of St Louis, in the thirteenth century, when Adam de la Halle wrote " Le Jeu de la Feuillée " and " Robin et Marion," the one a satire in dialogue, the other a pastoral comic opera. This Adam de la Halle was born in 1230. The fourteenth century has left but few plays, and Adam seems to have had no followers. Eustache Deschamp, however, mentions the theatre as a pastime adapted for women :—

> " Elles desirent les cités,
> Les douls mos a euls récités,
> Festes, marchiés et le theatre
> Lieux de delis pour euls esbatre."

Two comic plays are attributed to him, each having a special character, which cannot be connected with that of the following century. The first is a sort of morality; the second is a farce,—although neither bears either of these titles. The morality is called a "dit," written probably to serve as an interlude during some regal banquet. The "dits" were short poems, satiric or moral, belonging really to the didactic school. In the title it is, however, mentioned that they were to be performed by personages who were called "Débat," "Dispute," &c.

The farce entitled "Maitre Trubest et Antroignart" is a dialogue between a dishonest lawyer and a dishonest suitor. It is more of a fable than a play. The names of the personages are not mentioned, therefore we might reasonably suppose that a single person recited the different parts. These are the only instances of French comedy being mentioned in the fourteenth century. It would seem that between the reign of Philip III. (le Hardi) and Charles VII. (1422), there had been a complete interruption of theatrical literature, unless the comedies of that time have disappeared, for no trace of any works appears.

———

## FARCE.

THE word "farce" is easily traced from the Latin *farcire*, to stuff, to cram,—past participle *fartus* or *farsus*; *farsa* is the feminine gender. The farce, in liturgic language, was a sort of paraphrase mixed with the sacred text. Thus we read in old texts, "the kyrie eleison will be sung on the fête days with *farce*." These farces were, in the early times, no doubt moral and respectable in character; but in more modern times they must have degenerated, and led to abuse, since we see that the Bishop of Rouen (1248 to 1275), speaks of having interdicted the lessons with farces (*cum farcis*).

Although at a later period the farce conveyed no other idea than a merry comedy, often of a licentious kind, the origin of the word is the same whatever may have been its degenerate acceptation. Although it is not possible to fix the date when the word farce was first used in the acceptation just mentioned, and as it does not seem to have been thus employed anterior to the fifteenth century, we can but presume that farces may have existed before that kind of play was thus designated. No doubt it owes its influence to the *fables* or *dits*, as it began at the time when the latter ceased to be written. We may presume, that, although it borrowed its satire from the fable, together with its humorous and uncontrolled spirit, nevertheless it possesses a fund of comic power and originality entirely its own. These farces continued to be written with wonderful rapidity, and although many were destroyed in the Middle Ages, we can imagine what a vast number must have been produced, knowing that in every town many merry societies existed, who at certain times of the year—as far back as the seventeenth century—performed pieces, mostly farces. Many of these were probably never written out. They were invented with a view to amuse the public; they often were filled with a sort of local wit, calculated to cause laughter, without laying claim to any literary value.

Athough at times aggressive, the farce avoided the offence it might have given by its humorous bent. It says : " Ne vous fâchez pas ; je ris, je suis folle, ne vous donnez pas le ridicule de prendre un fou au sérieux." " Les Connards de Rouen," connards, or cornards,—thus called on account of the two horns or ears they wore on their fool's caps,—were strolling bands who travelled through the different districts reciting satirical poetry or performing farces. Their exertions were highly appreciated by the majority of the people, and they enjoyed such great privileges that their satire and insolence knew no bounds. Their chief had the title of abbot, and at Rouen, on days of festivity, he wore the mitre, enriched with precious stones (1509). Their satire on politics and religion was the cause of their ruin. The Calvinists united together against them, and interdicted their meetings (Rouen, 1562). Richelieu opposed them, and they were finally put down (1626 to 1636).

Another no less popular kind of entertainment was added to the

farce, namely " La Chanson." In the farce called " Le Savetier
Calbain," there are some twenty songs introduced. The farce
actors of that time could all sing, supplying by pantomimic action
what the voice could not render with effect.

## SOTTIES.

IT is supposed that in the reign of Charles II., towards the end
of the fourteenth century, a society was formed in Paris, composed of rich young men of good family, who called themselves
" Enfants sans souci." They also designated themselves " Sots."
The origin of the word is probably derived from the fact that
those young people acted all sorts of absurdities, representing and
ridiculing the different classes of society. The "sottie," or "sottise,"
was a farce acted by the "sots." These "sots," or "fol," had
their complete organisation, namely, its dignitaries, kings, middle
and lower class. Under the cloak of folly they ridiculed and
criticised the kings themselves. The "sot" wore a costume
somewhat similar to that of the king's fool, the principal feature
being a hood adorned with asses' ears and bells; he also carried
a fool's bauble. Yellow and green were the colours worn by a
"sot" and fool; the yellow signified gaiety, as a sort of
exhilarating virtue was attributed to saffron; green was the
symbol of hope, liberty, youth. Although traditions traced the
origin of the "sots" to a thoroughly organised society of rich
young gentlemen, we incline towards a different view; and judging
by the few documents left us, we believe them to have been a
company of poor youths, whose capital consisted entirely in their
wit, levity, unscrupulousness, and love for an idle and adventurous
life. In the fifteenth century, we see them described as
adventurers, or "la bohême" "du XVième siècle," and "d'insati-
ables affamés joyeux fainéants faméliques."

An interesting document, dating from the early part of the
sixteenth century, gives a sad description of the fortunes of the

"Enfants sans souci,"—"The Epitaph of the defunct 'Maistre Jehan Trotier'":—

> "Pleurz, pleurz, les enfants sans soucy,
> Quant vous voyez yey, moit et transy,
> Votre père, qui vous a gouvernez . . .
> Le bon Trotier qui longtemps a vescu
> Sans amasser ne grant blanc ne escu ;
> Mais soulement il voullut en son temps
> Cetre nommé l'un des pauvres contens :
> Faisant comme le bon lièvre chassé,
> Près de son giste est mort et trespassé,
> L'ouziesme jour de Janvier mil cinq cens."

Thus "le bon Trotier," probably the prince of the "sots," lived and died miserably. No doubt all his followers were in the same case. These idlers probably acquired their taste for the theatre and plays from the Basochiens, who were a society duly constituted, like most other corporations of the Middle Ages. It is stated, with more or less truth, that in 1303, Philippe le Bel gave the title of "Bayaume des Basochiens" to a society formed of the "Clercs du Parlement," who instituted a corporation for the protection of their mutual interests and common amusements. The term Basochiens is derived, according to some writers, from the Greek *basoqeios*—loquacious or talkative. Its derivation, however, comes more likely from the Greco-Latin word, *basilica*, a word applied to the royal courts of justice. From *basilica* came *basoche*, as *dimanche* comes from *dominica*. Until the middle of the sixteenth century, "les enfants sans souci" continued to enjoy the favour of the people, and were the main source of public amusement at the festivities held at Henry II.'s coronation. In 1559 they are supposed to have acted a farce called "Le Pauvre Villageois," before the court, on the occasion of the marriage of Madame Claude, daughter of Henry II., with Charles II. Duc of Lorraine.

The last traces of the "enfants sans souci" are found at the beginning of the seventeenth century, although the societies themselves had disappeared during the religious wars and violent

agitations which took place in Paris 1584-94, in the person of
Nicolas Joubert, who assumed the title of "Sieur d'Angoulevent,
prince des sots," and who died in 1615. After him there still
remained "des joeurs de farces," who performed farcical comedies,
clad in the fool's costume; and in 1616 we find a record of them
as having performed at the Hotel de Bourgogne. At that time,
however, there seems to have been some real actors. Pontalais,
in the reign of Francis I., in many ways resembles our modern
comic actors. Regular companies were formed with a respon-
sible manager; some of these companies received regular salaries,
others shared the receipts. This latter system of remuneration
by shares seems to have prevailed amongst actors, especially at
the beginning of the seventeenth century. Corneille exercised
his satirical wit on this sharing system, in his "Illusion comique,"
and concludes his remarks thus :—"On relève la toile et tous les
comédiens paraissent avec leur portier ; qui comptent l'argent sur
une table et prennent chacun leur part."

The French theatre, which is at present represented by the
Comèdie Française, is the result of long years of growth, as we
may see by tracing its origin to the reign of Henry IV., when
comedians founded the "Théatre du Marais." A few years later
another theatre was built, in a portion of the hotel of the
Dukes of Burgundy, in the Rue Mauconseil, called Hotel de
Bourgogne. This theatre was afterwards rendered celebrated
by Corneille, Rotrou, and Racine. Then again sprang up the
theatres of the "Petit Bourbon" and "Palais Royal," where
Racine's first piece, "La Thébaide," was produced, as well as
some of Molière's comedies. It is in the Hotel de Bourgogne
that plays by Corneille, Racine, and their predecessors were
originally performed. In 1680, that is seven years after the
death of Molière, we find three theatres in Paris, namely, "Le
Théatre du Marais," "l'Hotel de Bourgogne," and "Le Théatre
Guénégaud." Louis XIV. ordered the amalgamation of the two
principal companies, and incorporated them under the name of
"Comédie Française," thus creating a kind of parent institution
where literature as well as the art of acting found its own inspira-

tions. This Comédie Française, now called "Théatre Français," often changed its quarters; thus we find it migrating from the Palais Royal to the Rue Mazarin, then to the Rue des Fossés St-Germain in 1689. In this theatre were performed some pieces of Destouches, Crebillon, Lesage, Voltaire, Marivaux, Diderot, as well as others. From thence the Comédie took up its quarters at the Tuileries, where Beaumarchais had his "Barbier de Seville," and Voltaire his "Irene," represented. In 1782 the Odeon offered a new home to the company. The Comédie lived on until 1793, when the Revolution interrupted its course until 1799. Napoléon, as first consul, re-established it in its present home, Rue Richelieu. Until then the performances had been more primitive in style, for we hear of grandees occupying part of the stage, and sitting with their backs to the public all along the place where the footlights are now placed, thus interrupting the view of the pittites. At that time also the footlights consisted of candles, which had to be snuffed now and again during the performance. The monopoly given by the great king Louis XIV., and afterwards reconfirmed by Napoléon, made the present Comédie Française the greatest institution of the kind in the world. The general administrator is usually a distinguished man of letters; he works conjointly with some chosen members of the company, and several representatives of the State. The choice of these administrators is ratified by the "Ministre des beaux arts." This executive committee appoint the sociétaires, or members, from among the most distinguished individuals of the company. There are twenty-four sociétaires, who, after twenty years' service, are entitled to a pension of five thousand francs a year, with an increase of two hundred francs for each additional year. Without going into further details, these facts suffice to show the usefulness of such an institution. Authors, actors, and the public, are equally interested in its success, as it reflects a glorious past, and does honour to the country which gave it birth. A thousand pities that England, the cradle of tragedy, of literature, and the wealthiest country in the world, should not possess such an institution, and should allow its drama to shift

for itself as best it can, in the hands of private enterprise, and
to drift into those sensational exhibitions which interfere so
greatly with the love of the beautiful.

## ELIZABETH.

IN Italy the modern drama was developed earlier than in other
countries, and was supported by literary societies, who built
numerous theatres for the performance of plays before England
possessed any such buildings.  Sansovino and Titian built one of
the first theatres, at Canareggio, about 1570.  About the same
time, Palladio built a theatre at Carita, in which "Antigono," a
tragedy, written by the "Conte di Monte Vicentino," was represented.  The structure of these theatres, and of others such as
these built at Florence and Siena, resembled that of the ancient
amphitheatres.

In England, before the time of special theatres, tragedies were
performed in different halls of the Inns of Court, &c., fitted up
for these occasions.

The earliest known specimen of English tragedy is the play
of "Gorboduc; or, Ferrex and Porrex," written by Thomas
Sackville and Thomas Norton, and played before Queen Elizabeth
at Whitehall, by the members of the Inner Temple, on the 18th
of February 1561-62.  Shortly afterwards, Richard Edwards
(1523-66), a member of Lincoln's Inn and a popular poet, wrote
his classical drama of "Damon and Pythias," also "Palamon and
Arcite," which was performed before Queen Elizabeth in the hall
of Christ Church, Oxford.  During the first part of the performance, the scaffolding which supported the stage gave way, causing
the death of several persons and injury to many others.  The
stage, however, was repaired, and the performance went on.  The
Queen, who expressed herself highly gratified with the play, made
a present of eight pounds to one of the actors.  Many plays were
afterwards written and performed, and between the years 1568

and 1580, fifty-two dramas were acted before the court, under the superintendence of the master of the revels. The first regularly constructed theatre, in London, was opened at Blackfriars, in 1576; and in the beginning of Shakespeare's career five theatres were opened in London, besides other private establishments, which gave employment to a large number of actors. These theatres, of a circular form, were constructed of wood, and were partly open to the sky; the stage only had a thatched roof or covering; a flag was hoisted on the outside of it during the time of performance, which began at three o'clock, and was heralded by three blasts of the trumpet. (*See page* 277—Globe Theatre.)

The courtiers and their ladies, in the time of Queen Elizabeth, occupied boxes below the gallery, or sat on stools provided for them on the stage; whilst the younger gentlemen laid themselves down on the rush-strewn floor, attended by their servants, who handed them pipes of tobacco, considered at the time a great luxury. The commoners occupied the pit, or *yard*, which was not furnished with seats. Rude imitations of woods, houses, furniture, served as scenery; boards with large painted or written letters, indicating the localities where the action took place, were hung out during the performance. A dumb show or allegorical exhibition was displayed before each act, and gave an outline of what was to follow. Shakespeare, however, rarely employed this dumb show in his dramas or comedies. Female parts were performed by boys, or effeminate-looking young men; thus we may partly account for the coarseness of the speeches often put into the mouths of female characters in the old plays. This would strike us with a still greater sense of admiration for Shakespeare, who imparted to his female characters as much loveliness, exquisite refinement, or vigorous passions, as if the ladies themselves had been the performers. After each performance the clown of the company (or comic actor) recited or sung a jig, or a light humorous piece of writing :—

> " A jig shall be clapped at, and every rhyme
> Praised and applauded ; "
>
> (BEAUMONT.)

GLOBE THEATRE.

in which he introduced satires on public men and events, or made allusions to the audience. Before the public dispersed, all the actors came on the stage, and, kneeling, offered up a prayer for the Queen. It is not until after the Restoration (1660) that movable scenery was first introduced. This was done by Davenant, and actresses were now first seen on the stage.

If we compare the primitive and rude arrangements of the seventeenth century with more modern scenery and appliances, we must acknowledge that the actors of the present day have a great advantage over their predecessors in the display of their art. The lofty literature of our great dramatists, the sublime representations of characters by our great actors, have to some extent given place to the spectacular and pantomimic performances that have invaded our stage; and instead of causing in us that thrilling and ineffaceable sensation which genius never fails to awaken, the drama becomes simply the wonder of the moment, which the eye forgets almost as soon as it turns to another object.

In Dulwich College there is a memorandum written by the old theatrical manager Philip Henslowe, stating that the price he paid for a new play never exceeded £8,—that was in 1600; after that date he gave £20 and £25, in order to compete with rival companies. The proceeds of the second day's performance were also accorded to the author. Prologues for new plays rose in price from twenty to thirty shillings. The poverty of poets, although they may have been actors as well, was proverbial. In 1602 a sum of £10 was paid to Burbidge's players for performing " Othello " before Queen Elizabeth at Harefield, the seat of Sir Thomas Egerton; which shows that the managers of theatres derived a part of their income from private performances, while depending chiefly on public exhibitions. On the occasion of the first performance of " Othello," a bill was stuck on the entrance of the theatre, with the following matter printed in red letters:— " By Her Majesty's Company of Comedians. At the Globe Theatre this day will be acted a new tragedy called ' Othello, the Moor of Venice,' written by William Shakespeare. The play will begin at three o'clock exactly. Boxes, two shillings. Middle Gallery, one shilling. Upper Gallery and Pit, two pence."

## GERMAN DRAMA.

ALTHOUGH we have fully described the origin of the drama, and shown that it proceeded from the same causes in all civilised countries, yet it may not be without interest to cast a rapid glance at the sacred German dramas. The principal promoter of this form was Hans Sachs, who introduced a greater number of personages, and better scenery, than had been known in the mysteries and carnival farces performed by the artisans' guilds before his time (1494-1576). He revived in his plays the scriptural spirit which pervades the old mysteries, and especially drew from the Old Testament ; and the treatment is similar, inasmuch as he simply makes his personages relate, with action, the event he wishes to represent. In his plays he does not hesitate to mix up Christianity and heathendom. Many of his poems, although defaced by the coarseness of the time, were free from abuse or personality. His carnival play " Fastnachtspiel," which, it may be said, was the forerunner of the German drama, already existed in Nuremberg, and had been performed by the master-singers before him. He gave it a more refined form, investing it with satire and jest, avoiding at the same time the former outrageous merriment. From these carnival masqueradings, buffoonery, and tirades, came this miracle play. It represented the circumstances of ordinary life, with its quarrels, friendships, &c. The jokes made at the cost of the Church were always full of good and genial humour. The apostles were familiarly introduced, but not without respect. In the carnival play, St Peter obtains permission of the Lord to take a formal farewell of his friends. He says :—

> " Good Lord, I pray thee, grant to me,
> If every wise it well may be,
> That for just three days I may go
> Once more to dwell on earth below ;
> For three short days my friends to see,
> And feast once more right merrily."

*A. W. Jackson's Translation of Carl Hase.*

While he is away the gate of heaven may remain closed ; Peter
promises to see that it is properly shut. After meeting with
friends, Peter reappears in another scene, suffering from headache
after a sojourn of a few days. This reminds him of his promise,
and whilst ascending to heaven, he is met by the Lord, who
has come forth to watch for him. Peter craves forgiveness, and
explains that jollity and good cheer had kept him longer than the
permitted time. He is then asked if all his friends were filled
with gratitude towards the Lord for the blessings showered upon
them. Peter is then obliged to confess that no one ever mentioned the name of God, except an old woman, who screamed
and implored the Lord to help her whilst her goods were burn-
ing,—which caused general laughter. After a second visit to the
earth, for which permission is again granted to him, he returns
hurriedly to heaven, and answers the Lord, who once more questions him :—

> "Is there still none who asks for Me ?"

### PETER.

> "Oh, yes, most gracious Lord ! for Thee
> Both young and old with fervour cry ;
> Early and late they weep and sigh,
> In penitence would pity win ;
> Owning, with grief, their guilt and sin
> With such true heart their cry they make,
> Return, O Lord ! sweet pity take !
> To heal and end their bitter pain,
> Myself, I cry, Lord, turn again !"
>
> —*A. W. Jackson.*

The Lord finding after Peter's first visit that mortals did not
trouble about Him, had sent plagues and destruction on earth
before Peter's second descent.

Hans Sachs was a shoemaker at Nuremberg, and managed
to acquire a certain amount of classical training at a Latin school.
He travelled through different towns, and at Munich he studied
with his fellow-townsman Nunnenbeck, and at Frankfort he
frequented the singing-school of the Meistersingers. It was at
the beginning of the fourteenth century that Germany witnessed

the first formation of those brotherhoods composed of poet-artisans. They practised the poetical art, according to certain strict rules of prosody,—although such pedantic rules did not in any way affect the measurement of the verses. They met in taverns, where their poems were read out. Apprentices, journeymen, and masters made up these societies. The title of master could not be obtained without a knowledge of music ; as, to compose different airs for the written poetry, was a necessary accomplishment. Charles IV. (1378), and Maximilian afterwards granted many privileges to these guilds. To Hans Sachs are attributed 6,048 pieces, including psalms, the Song of Solomon, 26 sacred comedies, 27 sacred plays, 52 secular comedies, 28 secular tragedies, 64 carnival farces, 59 fables, 116 allegorical fables, 307 poems secular and sacred, and 197 comic tales.

Gotthold - Ephraim Lessing, born in January 1729 at Kamenz, a small town in Lusatia, may be considered as having rendered the greatest services to German dramatic literature. His father was a Protestant clergyman, a man of learning. He studied at Leipsic, and attended Koestner's lectures, which greatly contributed to develop in him the germs of his great talent. He had an innate love for the stage, and through his intercourse with actors, made himself acquainted with many details of their art, which dramatic authors cannot ignore without detriment to their works. The first play which appeared under his name is called "Le Jeune Savant," "The Young Scholar." It met with the approval of the public, and of Weisse, an eminent writer of the time. This greatly encouraged Lessing in his course ; and shortly after his arrival in Berlin he published his memoirs and contributions to the history and appreciation of the stage, "Beytræge zur Historie und Aufnahme des Theaters." Then followed the "Kleinigkeiten" Trifles, &c., &c. When his first work came out, German literature was yet in its infancy; since Opitz, Logan, and others, few important works had appeared. The "Messiah" by Klopstock, Kleist's "Spring," and certain light works by Lichtwehr, Hagedorn, &c., although forming a certain epoch, yet did not constitute a literature. The predilections of Frederick II. for French literature, the works of Voltaire especially, delayed the progress of German literature. Gottsched, who was prominent as a writer, made it too subservient to the Greek and French models, regardless of the genius of his own country. Wieland was the first who translated Shakespeare. He and Lessing, who praised the translation, really revealed the existence of the great English poet to the German nation, for English literature was almost ignored at that time. Lessing's influence showed itself first on the stage. His early productions were, besides "The Young Scholar," "The Jews," "The Misogynist" (the woman-hater), "The Freethinker." These plays, written by a young man twenty years of age, who had only just left school, were full of coarse jokes, interspersed now and then with clever traits, yet the dialogue was an improvement on the usual form of writing. "Miss Sarah Sampson" (1755) and "Philotas" (1759) showed a great improvement, and the latter especially displayed heroic sentiments and beauty of style. "Minna von Barnhelm" (1763) is an advance on his other plays, and shows the German habits and customs, which he delineates heartily and with well-designed characters. His tragedy "Emilia Galotti" (1772), with some of his other works, may be considered as having greatly perfected the German style of writing. Lessing never was surpassed by his contemporaries, and equalled by very few of his successors. His writing may be compared to that of our best authors.

The full development and the highest flight of German drama were attained in the period of Goethe and Schiller. Johann Wolfgang Goethe (1749-1832) was justly called the "all-sided," from the infinite variety of his literary productions, and this applies also to his dramatic activity. In his "Iphigenia" is reproduced the very spirit of Greek tragedy; his "Götz von Berlichingen" reminds us in its construction of the "histories" of Shakespeare, and especially of that play which describes the War of the Roses. In his "Egmont" he gives us the sunny heroism of the Flemish noble, in brilliant contrast with the dark intrigues of the gloomy Spanish court. His "Faust" sounds every chord of human emotion and passion; and in his lighter works, such as his "Bürgergeneral," he sports with the humorous and eccentric side of human nature. Friedrich von Schiller (1759-1806) was greatest in historic drama. His "Wallenstein"—a noble trilogy— has been pronounced by Carlyle the greatest dramatic work of the eighteenth century. In his "William Tell" he advocates the principles of free government against the tyranny of feudalism; his "Maid of Orleans" gives a brilliant and imaginative picture of the most romantic episode in French history; and in "Don Carlos" we have a vivid picture of the priest-ridden king, who crushed the life out of the magnificent inheritance he was called upon to govern. The late German dramatists generally modelled their work upon Goethe and Schiller. The one drama which has become popular in England is the "Son of the Wilderness," of Münch-Bellinghausen, who wrote under the pseudonym of Friedrich Halm. This play, under the name of the chief character, "Ingomar," has been frequently produced, in an English garb, on the stage in England and America.

## THE CHINESE THEATRE.

THE Chinese theatre of the present day has not, according to reliable accounts given by competent writers, developed into scenic perfection, like the European theatres. Its condition rather resembles the primitive state that existed in England in the early part of the seventeenth century. A stage of boards, raised on tressels seven or eight feet high, painted canvas at the sides and back, and a rustic roof or covering, constitute the scene. Round it are built raised planks, as we see in "penny shows." No scenery, only a few wooden stools to represent furniture. Such is the present theatre in China. There are no buildings especially devoted to theatrical purposes; so that to have a performance the inhabitants of a district subscribe the necessary funds to cover the expenses, and at a short notice this rough sort of structure is put up in a public square or street.

The performances take place for the benefit of the general public, and are in some degree encouraged by the Mandarins, who add their subscription to the general fund. The higher class of performances are to be witnessed in the houses of the rich and of the aristocracy, in whose houses a stage is generally erected. Not only is it customary to invite friends and equals, but a certain amount of room is also reserved for the general public. It is in these gatherings that classical works are witnessed, and they are much appreciated by a cultured public, although they are without any of the scenic effects which play so important a part in our present performances. We see by these facts that the Chinese habits and inclinations do not always lean to the beating of drums and gongs, and blowing of toy trumpets, especially in those receptions where classics and literary works form the sole attraction.

The same state of things exists in China that used to prevail in Europe centuries ago. Comedians are considered as a sort of outcasts, and belong to a low class of society. They are strollers, and travel from town to town; they have their chiefs, and, like tribes, have their laws. Only some of the largest and wealthiest towns possess theatres, with regular troops of actors attached to them. These exceptional theatres are properly erected buildings, where entertainments of a higher class are given. There are no actresses in China, female parts being assumed by young men. Formerly, under the rule of the Mongolian emperors, there were actresses. In 1263, Khoublai issued a decree, by which actresses were considered as belonging to the lowest and most degraded class of women. Probably the contempt in which they were held caused so much irregularity of behaviour amongst them, that it was thought necessary to banish them from the stage altogether. This measure was taken as lately as in the last century.

In the banquets that are given on days of reception; the guests are seated two by two at each table, that they may see what is going on on the stage. The servants bring in different dishes, the feast consisting of sixteen or eighteen courses. As soon as the actors appear, the most profound silence prevails. The performers are richly clad, and on entering the room they bow together. One of them is led to the most distinguished guest, and presents him with a book, in which are inscribed in golden letters some fifty or sixty plays, which the comedians know by heart, and any one of which they are able to perform at once. The book is passed round among the guests, and when the choice of a piece has been made, the doors are opened, and the public is admitted to the part of the room reserved for that purpose. The lady of the house and her friends have their seats in a gallery apart, and hidden by a sort of grating.

The entertainments of the Chinese are no less original than their eccentric dishes. An amusing tale is related in connection with a banquet given in honour of Lord Macartney, the English envoy, and his suite, during that nobleman's embassy to China. After many suspicious courses had been allowed to pass untouched by our Englishmen, some of his excellency's aides de camp fancied an entrée of inviting appearance, that looked like a salmi of a kind of bird. They tried it, and found it sufficiently relishing to compensate them for their prudent abstemiousness. Wishing to know what the ingredients of the dish might really be, one of the Englishmen turned to a Chinese attendant, and in the belief that the platter had contained some preparation of duck, pointed to it, and said inquiringly—"Quack, quack, quack?" But the Chinaman shook his head, and with the child-like and bland smile characteristic of his countrymen, answered—"Bow, wow, wow!"

The Chinese being perhaps less given to indulge the imagination and to violent passion than the European nations, their plays deal generally with the ordinary circumstances and events of life, and are seldom based on love intrigues. The Chinese drama resembles the European dramas so far as the division of the scenes and acts is concerned. A play in three acts and a prologue corresponds to three acts and an overture. In high-class dramas the sentiments are of an elevated character. For instance, motherly or filial love, zeal for the study of literature, sense of honour, &c.,

predominate. There are also comedies of minor importance, in
which low intrigues are introduced. A striking difference exists
between the Chinese theatre and the European drama in the part
of the singer.

In French vaudevilles a few songs are introduced, of a light
character, and these add to the variety of the entertainment,
without forming an essential part of the plot. On the Chinese
stage, *one* person only sings. The singer takes part in the action,
and is the interpreter of moral sentiments ; he also explains to the
public the intricacies of the different situations, after the manner
of the Greek chorus. The singer is accompanied by instruments,
probably played in a sort of symphonic effect, much appreciated
by those who have the privilege of witnessing these performances.
It is said that the Chinese are fond of good music, and when an
Italian troupe of operatic singers executed some of Rossini's
works at Macao in 1833, the spectators expressed their astonishment to hear recitatives and melodies so much like their own.
Our experience of Chinese music probably conveys to our ears a
very inadequate idea of the manner in which the senses of the
natives may be pleased at the performance of music properly
rendered, especially in a class of society where poetry and high-
class literature are widely cultivated.

THE DARIEN PRESS, BRISTO PLACE, EDINBURGH.

LaVergne, TN USA
15 March 2011
220053LV00001B/2/A